REPTILE REALM

1000 Super Wild Facts About Snakes and Lizards

Nicole Foster

PRECAUTIONARY NOTE

While every precaution has been taken in the preparation of this book, the publisher assumes no responsibility for errors, omissions, or damages resulting from using the information contained herein. First edition. 17th April 2023. Copyright © 2023 Grammatika Press. Written by Nicole Foster. Illustrated by Senarath Dharmatilake.

DISCLAIMER

© **Copyright 2023 Nicole Foster** - All rights reserved. The content contained within this book may not be reproduced, duplicated, or transmitted without direct written permission from the author or the publisher. Under no circumstances will any blame or legal responsibility be held against the publisher, or author, for any damages, reparation, or monetary loss due to the information contained within this book, either directly or indirectly.

Legal Notice: This book is copyright protected. This book is only for personal use. You cannot amend, distribute, sell, use, quote, or paraphrase any part, or the content within this book, without the author's or publisher's consent.

Disclaimer Notice: Please note the information contained within this document is for educational and entertainment purposes only. All effort has been executed to present accurate, up-to-date, and reliable, complete information. No warranties of any kind are declared or implied. Readers acknowledge that the author is not rendering legal, financial, medical, or professional advice.

By reading this document, the reader agrees that under no circumstances is the author responsible for any losses, direct or indirect, which are incurred as a result of the use of the information contained within this document, including, but not limited to errors, omissions, or inaccuracies.

CONTENTS

SNAKES: AN IN-DEPTH EXPLORATION

INTRODUCTION	3
PHYSIOLOGY OF SNAKES: HOW THEIR BODIES FUNCTION	5
SNAKES AROUND THE WORLD (LOCATION)	13
Types of snakes	17
CLASSIFICATION OF SNAKES	20
WHICH COUNTRY HAS THE DEADLIEST SNAKES?	26
Some Fun Facts About the Black Mamba	32
King Cobra: The Majestic Monarch of the Snake World	35
CATCHING PREY	39
Venomous and non-venomous snakes	39
How to identify venomous snakes	41
Snake bites to humans	47
What do snake bites do to the human body?	48
What should a human do if bitten by a snake?	50
How do venomous snakes kill their prey?	50
How do non-venomous snakes kill their prey?	52
Can a python kill a human?	54
What to do if you see a snake	56
Eating Facts	57
How do they eat	58
How exactly do snakes eat and digest?	60
How long do snakes go without eating?	62
REPRODUCTION AND LIFE CYCLE	64
Reproductive strategies of snakes	65
Courtship and mating behavior	69

Egg-Laying and Incubation in Snakes	71
Egg-Laying Process:	71
Egg Structure and Composition:	72
Incubation:	72
Parental Care during Incubation:	73
Hibernation	74
More Snakey Facts	76
FAMOUS SNAKE STORIES	79
The Cleopatra Incident	79
The Ophidiophobia Incident	80
Snake Island	81
The Medusa Incident	81
The South African Incident	81
The Australian incident	82
Famous snake handlers	83
Wild extra random facts about snakes' bodies	91
CONCLUSION	97

LIZARDS: AN IN-DEPTH EXPLORATION

INTRODUCTION	101
WHAT'S A LIZARD?	103
General Facts about Lizards	104
BEHAVIOR OF LIZARDS	108
GEOGRAPHICAL DISTRIBUTION OF LIZARDS	114
Adaptations of lizards to different environments	118
TYPES OF LIZARDS	127
WILD FACTS ABOUT THEIR BODIES	136
Lizards and Poison/venom	148
PREDATORS THAT AFFECT LIZARDS	150
CATCHING FOOD AND FOOD FACTS	152
How do they eat?	152

LIZARDS IN THE NEWS	154
Komodo Island: Home of the World's Largest Lizards	154
Komodo Dragons in the news	155
Thanks	157
References	159

DEDICATION

To all the curious minds and passionate herpetologists who have dedicated their lives to unraveling the secrets of these magnificent creatures, this book is a tribute to your relentless pursuit of knowledge and understanding. May this book inspire a new generation of reptile enthusiasts, fostering a deep appreciation and respect for the incredible diversity and beauty that the world of snakes and lizards has to offer. Let us continue to learn, share, and celebrate the wonders of these fascinating creatures that have captivated our imaginations and enriched our planet for millions of years.

Xavier Chacon, this book is for you.

SNAKES: AN IN-DEPTH EXPLORATION

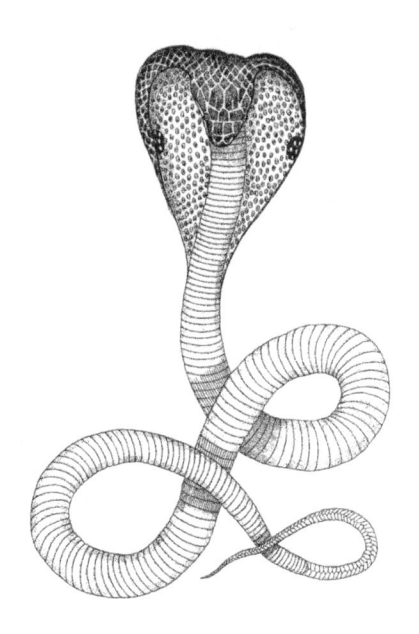

Cobra

INTRODUCTION

Snakes are one of the most captivating creatures on Earth. They can be found in almost every part of the world, from the deserts of Australia to the rainforests of South America. They come in varying shapes and sizes, and some can be incredibly deadly. But despite their reputation, snakes are truly amazing animals that have adapted to survive in some of the harshest environments on the planet.

In this book, we'll take a journey through the world of snakes. We'll explore the different types of snakes, from the harmless garden snake to the deadly king cobra. We'll examine their physiology and share some wild and fascinating facts about their bodies. We'll look at how venomous and non-venomous snakes catch their prey and learn see what happens when a snake bites a human.

We'll also delve into the eating habits of snakes, including how they eat and how long they can go without food. We'll explore how they hibernate and what predators they have in the wild. We'll also discuss how they protect themselves, from camouflaging to hissing and rattling their tails.

Finally, we'll share some famous snake stories from around the world, from the Cleopatra incident to the Irula tribe in India, who catch snakes for a living. We'll also look at famous snake handlers, including Steve Irwin's "The Crocodile Hunter."

Throughout this book, you'll discover a world of fascinating information about snakes. Whether you're a snake enthusiast or just looking to learn more about these incredible creatures, this book is the perfect guide to help you explore the world of snakes. So, let's slither our way through the world of snakes and uncover some of the most interesting and exciting facts about these fascinating animals.

PHYSIOLOGY OF SNAKES: HOW THEIR BODIES FUNCTION

🐍 Snakes are a varied group of reptiles with a unique body structure that sets them apart from other animals.

🐍 Their distinct adaptations have allowed them to live happily in a variety of environments across the globe.

🐍 In this section, we will explore the captivating world of snake physiology, looking into their skeletal structure, muscular system, body sensory organs, and other remarkable features that make these creatures truly extraordinary.

Skeletal Structure:

🐍 One of the most striking features of snakes is their long body without limbs.

🐍 They have a skeletal structure that allows for excellent movement and flexibility.

🐍 The snake's spine has many back bones (vertebrae), and each vertebra is connected to a pair of ribs.

🐍 This high number of vertebrae (ranging from 200 to 400 back bones depending on the species) allows the snake to be highly flexible, enabling it to move through tight spaces and pass through difficult landscapes.

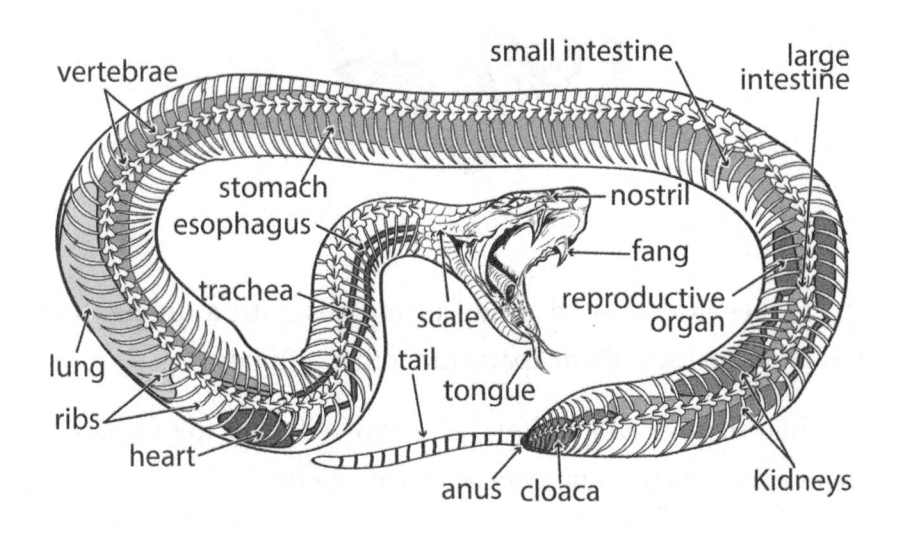

Diagram labels: vertebrae, small intestine, large intestine, stomach, esophagus, nostril, fang, trachea, reproductive organ, scale, lung, tail, ribs, tongue, heart, anus, cloaca, Kidneys

Muscular System:

🐍 The snake's muscular system is equally impressive, with a combination of dorsal (back of the body), ventral (front of the body), and lateral (side) muscles working together to accelerate movement.

🐍 These muscles let snakes contract and expand their body, allowing them to move in a variety of ways, such as sidewinding (the curling way they move on the floor), concertina movement (the curling way they move and then straighten), and the more familiar rolling motion known as serpentine movement (the 'S' shape.)

🐍 The snake's muscles also play a crucial role in constriction, a hunting technique some species use to squeeze and subdue their prey by wrapping their body around the victim and applying pressure.

Respiratory System:

🐍 Snakes have only one working lung (usually the right one).

🐍 The other lung doesn't work or is absent altogether.

🐍 Even with just a single lung, snakes have developed an efficient way of receiving oxygen from the air.

🐍 They have a long trachea (windpipe) extending almost the entire body length to provide air exchange.

🐍 Snakes can also breathe while swallowing large prey, thanks to a special extension of their windpipe called the glottis.

🐍 They can move the glottis to the side during feeding.

Digestive System:

🐍 The snake's digestive system is highly specialized for its complex diet, typically consisting of large, whole animals as prey.

🐍 Snakes have an elastic stomach and an expandable esophagus that allows them to swallow prey much larger than their own head.

- Once swallowed, powerful digestive enzymes break down the prey. At the same time, the snake's slow metabolism ensures that it can go for extended periods between meals.

- In some cases, a snake may only need to eat a few times a year.

Sensory Organs:

- Snakes have a range of sensory organs that help them move across their environment and locate prey.

- Their eyesight isn't excellent, but their eyes have adapted to detect movement.

- Some species have holes inside their face between the eyes and the nostrils, known as pit organs.

- These highly evolved pit organs allow them to detect the heat signatures of warm-blooded prey.

- The pit organs are like infrared cameras at night, allowing the snakes to 'see' the prey.

- Snakes have nostrils but smell through their tongues.

- Some snakes can smell a little bit through their nostrils, but odors are mainly smelt through the tongue.

- They use their forked tongue to collect scents from the air, which goes to the Jacobson's organ, a specialized structure that receives smells in the roof of their mouth.

SNAKES: AN IN-DEPTH EXPLORATION

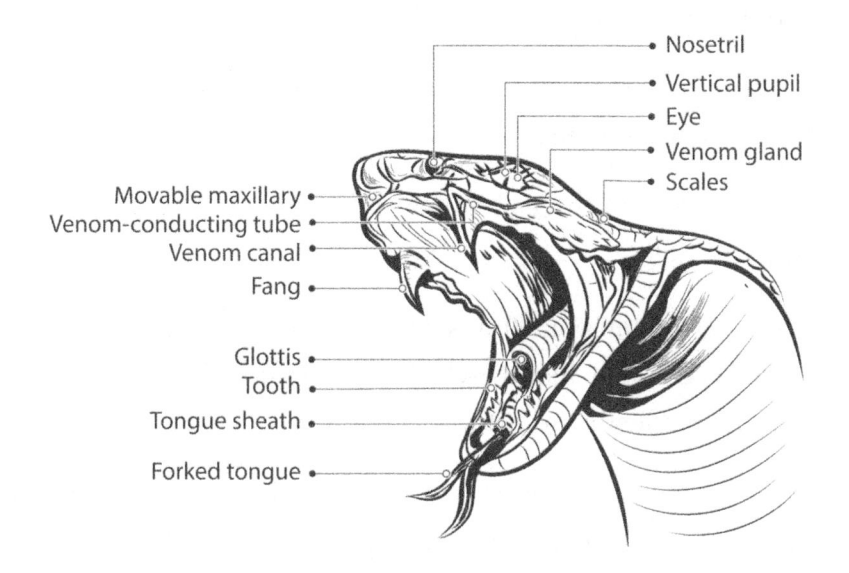

- Nosetril
- Vertical pupil
- Eye
- Venom gland
- Scales
- Movable maxillary
- Venom-conducting tube
- Venom canal
- Fang
- Glottis
- Tooth
- Tongue sheath
- Forked tongue

Thermoregulation:

🐍 Snakes are ectothermic animals, meaning they need external heat sources to regulate their body temperature.

🐍 This means they must actively look for warmer or cooler environments to maintain an ideal temperature range for their bodily processes.

🐍 Snakes often lie in the sun to warm up or go to shaded areas or burrows to cool down.

🐍 Finding the ideal regulation for their body temperature is incredibly important.

🐍 This thermoregulatory behavior is essential to their daily activities, affecting their metabolism, digestion, and overall energy levels.

Circulatory System:

🐍 The circulatory system of snakes is completely different from that of mammals.

🐍 Snakes have a three-chambered heart with two atria and a single ventricle.

🐍 This arrangement allows for some mixing of oxygenated and deoxygenated blood, which is well-suited to the snake's slower metabolism and ectothermic lifestyle.

🐍 The snake's circulatory system also plays a major role in snakes being able to swallow large prey.

🐍 As the snake ingests its meal, its heart can shift position to allow the expanding esophagus to ensure that blood flows normally while the snake swallows the prey.

Excretory System:

🐍 Snakes have a pair of long kidneys that filter waste from the blood.

🐍 Their feces and urine are mixed together in much the same way as birds.

🐍 This allows snakes to keep extra water in their bodies if they need to adapt to an environment.

🐍 The waste from their body is excreted through an area called the cloaca. The cloaca is an opening at the end of a snake's belly where the tail begins.

🐍 Snakes also lay eggs and mate through this same opening.

🐍 A snake usually 'goes to the toilet' every 5-8 days.

Skin and Molting:

🐍 Many people think snakes would be slimy to the touch, but it is quite the opposite.

🐍 The skin of snakes is covered in scales, which protects them from predators, provides moisture retention, and helps with movement across rough landscapes.

🐍 Snakes often shed their skin in a process called molting or ecdysis.

🐍 As a snake's body grows, the skin does not, so this is why a snake sheds so often.

🐍 Snakes can also get parasites and bugs attached to their skin, which is uncomfortable – so they just shed it.

🐍 This shedding process allows the snake to replace old, damaged skin with a fresh layer.

🐍 Before shedding, a snake's skin becomes dull, and a milky fluid is secreted between the old and new skin layers.

🐍 The snake will then rub against rough surfaces to loosen the old skin, eventually peeling it off in one continuous piece to reveal the new skin.

🐍 Shedding can take one to two weeks and can be extremely stressful for the snake.

🐍 Snakes have eye caps instead of eyelids. If these caps do not shed, the snake can go completely blind.

🐍 A snake will usually shed its skin close to their habitat where they live. So if you see a skin at home, get a snake catcher!

Coloration and Camouflage:

🐍 Snakes have a wide variety of colors and patterns, which serve different purposes depending on the species.

🐍 Some snakes have adapted their colors to help them blend into their surroundings, making it difficult for predators to spot them.

🐍 This also means the prey cannot detect them, which is perfect for the snake. The prey may be just crossing a rocky area, but the snake is part of that landscape.

🐍 Other snakes display bright, contrasting colors and intricate patterns like diamonds.

🐍 These bright colors serve as a warning to potential predators that they are venomous.

🐍 Some non-venomous species even copy the appearance of venomous snakes to keep predators away. This is a phenomenon known as Batesian mimicry.

🐍 However, there are many deadly, venomous snakes without colors and patterns.

SNAKES AROUND THE WORLD (LOCATION)

🐍 Snakes can be found in almost every part of the world, from the deserts of Australia to the rainforests of South America.

🐍 There are no snakes in Antarctica, though.

🐍 Let's take a look at some of the most notable locations where snakes can be found around the world:

North America:

🐍 In North America, snakes can be found in a wide range of habitats, from deserts to forests to wetlands.

🐍 Some of the most common species in North America include the garter snake, the corn snake, and the copperhead snake.

🐍 The rattlesnake is also found in North America and is known for its distinctive rattle that warns potential predators of its presence.

South America:

🐍 South America is home to some of the most fascinating snakes in the world, including the anaconda, the bushmaster, and the boa constrictor.

🐍 The anaconda is one of the largest snakes in the world and can grow up to 30 feet long.

🐍 The bushmaster is also a large and deadly snake found in South America's rainforests.

Africa:

🐍 Africa is home to some of the most venomous snakes in the world, including the black mamba, the boomslang, and the puff adder.

Puff Adder

- The black mamba is known for its speed and agility and is considered one of the deadliest snakes in the world.

- More about the black mamba later on in this book.

- The 2-meter boomslang is also venomous and is known for its potent venom that can cause hemorrhaging and other severe symptoms.

- The boomslang is a beautiful-looking snake and often has a bright green belly and a pink or orange throat. If you see one, run.

Asia:

- Asia is home to some of the most diverse snake populations in the world, with species ranging from the king cobra to the green tree snake.

- The king cobra is one of the most iconic snakes in Asia and is known for its deadly venom and impressive size.

- The green tree snake is a non-venomous species found throughout Southeast Asia and is known for its striking green coloration.

Australia:

- Australia has over 170 snake species, and 20 of the 25 deadliest snakes live in Australia.

- Eleven (11) of the world's deadliest snakes can be found in Australia.

🐍 It is home to the inland taipan, which is the world's most venomous snake.

🐍 The inland taipan's venom can cause paralysis and death within minutes.

🐍 The inland taipan is found nowhere else on Earth.

🐍 Australia also has the coastal taipan, the eastern and western brown snakes, and the king brown. These are responsible for a large number of snakebite deaths in Australia each year.

🐍 Other deadly snakes include the tiger snake, copperhead snake, and the deadly 50cm long, small-eyed snake.

Tiger Snake

Europe:

🐍 Europe is home to many snake species, including the viper, the grass snake, and the adder.

🐍 The viper is a venomous species throughout Europe and Asia known for its distinctive zigzag pattern.

🐍 The grass snake is a non-venomous species found throughout Europe and is known for its striking green coloration.

TYPES OF SNAKES

🐍 Snakes come in all shapes, sizes, and colors.

🐍 They are fascinating creatures that have captured the imagination of humans for centuries.

🐍 There are more than 3,500 species of snakes worldwide, ranging from tiny thread snakes that are only a few inches long to massive pythons that can grow up to 30 feet long.

🐍 One way to classify snakes is by their physical characteristics. For example, some snakes are venomous, while others are not.

🐍 Venomous snakes have glands that produce venom, which they use to kill their prey or defend themselves from predators. Some examples of venomous snakes include the cobra, rattlesnake, and black mamba.

🐍 Another way to classify snakes is by their habitat. Some snakes live in trees, while others live on the ground. Some snakes live in water, while others live in deserts or rainforests. For example, the anaconda lives in the water, while the king cobra lives on land.

🐍 Snakes can also be classified by their behavior. For instance, some snakes are nocturnal, which means they are most active at night. Others are diurnal, which means they are most active during the day. Some snakes are solitary, while others live in groups.

🐍 There are also different types of snakes based on their diet. Some snakes eat only insects, while others eat small mammals like koalas or reptiles.

🐍 Some snakes are specialists and eat only one type of prey. In contrast, others are generalists and will eat a wide variety of prey. Following are seven examples of snakes and their diets:

1. Insectivorous snakes: These snakes feed exclusively on insects, such as crickets, beetles, and grasshoppers. Examples of insectivorous snakes include the sharp-tailed snake and the thread snake.

2. Carnivorous snakes: These snakes eat other animals, such as rodents, birds, and other reptiles. Some examples of carnivorous snakes include the king cobra, which feeds on other snakes, and the rattlesnake, which feeds on small mammals like rodents.

3. Piscivorous snakes: These snakes feed on fish and other aquatic animals. Examples of piscivorous snakes include the water snake and the sea snake.

4. Ophiophagous snakes: These snakes specialize in eating other snakes. Examples of ophiophagous snakes include the king snake and the black racer.

5. Frugivorous snakes: These snakes feed extensively on fruit as well as prey. Examples of frugivorous snakes include the paradise tree snake and the green tree python.

6. Vermivorous snakes: These snakes eat earthworms and other small invertebrates. Examples of vermivorous snakes include the earth snake and the worm snake.

7. Myrmecophagous snakes: These snakes feed on ants and other social insects. Examples of myrmecophagous snakes include the black-headed snake and the western shovel-nosed snake.

CLASSIFICATION OF SNAKES

🐍 Snakes are a diverse group of reptiles belonging to the suborder Serpentes, which fall under the order Squamata, containing lizards and snakes.

🐍 There are approximately 3,600 known species of snakes, which are classified into several families based on their shared morphological, genetic, and ecological characteristics.

🐍 In this section, we will delve into the classification of snakes, exploring the 9 different families and providing examples of species from each group.

1. Typhlopidae (Blind Snakes):

🐍 Typhlopidae, also known as worm snakes or blind snakes, has around 260 species.

🐍 These small, burrowing snakes are found chiefly in tropical and subtropical regions around the world.

- They have small eyes covered by scales, which is why they are called "blind" snakes.
- They primarily feed on insects, particularly ants and termites.
- Examples of blind snakes include the brahminy blind snake and the Texas blind snake.

2. Boidae (Boas):

- The Boidae family contains around 60 species of boas, which are non-venomous, constricting snakes.
- They squeeze their prey to death.
- They are found across the Americas, Africa, Europe, and parts of Asia.
- Boas are known for their robust bodies and strong, muscular constriction used to subdue their prey.
- Some well-known species in this family include the boa constrictor, the green anaconda, and the emerald tree boa.

3. Pythonidae (Pythons):

- The Pythonidae family consists of approximately 40 species of pythons, which are non-venomous, constricting snakes native to Africa, Asia, and Australia.
- Pythons are known for their large size and striking patterns, making them popular among reptile enthusiasts.
- Some notable examples include the reticulated python

(Malayopython reticulatus), the burmese python (Python bivittatus), and the ball python (Python regius).

4. Colubridae (Colubrids):

🐍 The Colubridae family is the largest family of snakes, having around 1,900 species.

🐍 Colubrids are found worldwide, except for Antarctica, and exhibit a wide range of sizes, colors, and behaviors.

🐍 Most Colubrids are non-venomous or have venom that is harmless to humans.

🐍 Examples of Colubrid snakes include the corn snake (Pantherophis guttatus), the king snake (Lampropeltis getula), and the boomslang (Dispholidus typus).

🐍 There are exceptions to being harmless to humans, though. The boomslang is a killer for humans.

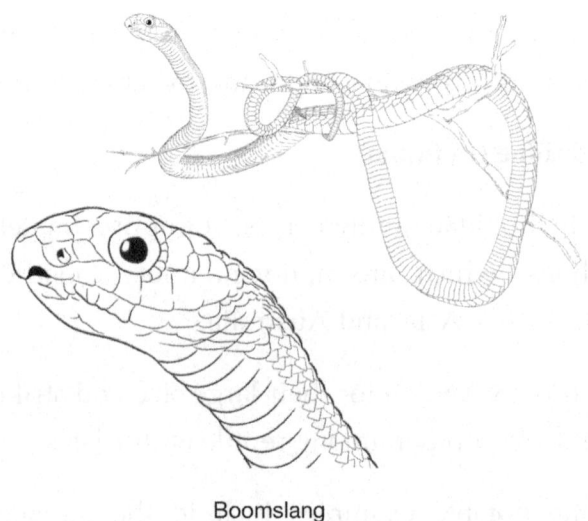

Boomslang

SNAKES: AN IN-DEPTH EXPLORATION

5. Elapidae (Elapids):

🐍 The Elapidae family consists of approximately 360 species of venomous snakes, including some of the world's most dangerous and recognizable snakes. Elapids have hollow, fixed fangs through which they deliver their potent venom.

🐍 They are found primarily in tropical and subtropical regions of the world, such as Africa, Asia, Australia, and the Americas.

🐍 Examples of Elapid snakes include the king cobra (Ophiophagus Hannah), the black mamba (Dendroaspis polylepis), and the many species of coral snakes (Micrurus spp.).

6. Viperidae (Vipers and Pit Vipers):

🐍 The Viperidae family comprises around 340 species of venomous snakes, including vipers and pit vipers.

🐍 Vipers are characterized by their long, hinged fangs that can fold back when not in use.

🐍 Pit vipers, a subfamily within Viperidae called Crotalinae, have a unique heat-sensing organ called a "pit" located between their eyes and nostrils, which helps them detect warm-blooded prey.

🐍 Viperidae species are found in various regions worldwide, including Europe, Asia, Africa, and the Americas.

🐍 Examples of snakes in this family include the European adder (Vipera berus), the gaboon viper (Bitis gabonica), and the rattlesnakes (Crotalus spp.).

🐍 Did you know when vipers are born, they can hunt and defend themselves immediately after birth?

7. Lamprophiidae (African House Snakes and Allies):

🐍 The Lamprophiidae family contains around 330 species, predominantly found in Africa and parts of Europe and Asia.

🐍 Lamprophiids show varied appearances and behaviors, ranging from small, secretive snakes to large, robust species.

🐍 Most lamprophiids are non-venomous or have venom that is not dangerous to humans.

🐍 Examples of snakes in this family include the african house snake (Boaedon fuliginosus), the spotted bush snake (Philothamnus semivariegatus), and the mole snake (Pseudaspis cana).

8. Natricidae (Water Snakes and Allies):

🐍 The Natricidae family includes approximately 230 species, found mainly in North America, Europe, Africa, and Asia.

🐍 Many Natricids live in or near aquatic habitats, such as rivers, lakes, and wetlands, and are expert swimmers.

🐍 Most species in this family are non-venomous or have venom that is harmless to humans.

🐍 Examples of Natricid snakes include the common garter snake (Thamnophis sirtalis), the European grass snake (Natrix natrix), and the keelback (Rhabdophis spp.).

9. Dipsadidae (South and Central American Snakes):

🐍 The Dipsadidae family is a diverse group of around 800 species, primarily found in South and Central America. However, some species can also be found in the southern United States and the Caribbean.

🐍 Dipsadids display a variety of forms, colors, and behaviors and include both venomous and non-venomous species. Examples of dipsadid snakes include the green vine snake (Oxybelis fulgidus), the mussurana (Clelia clelia), and the bird snake (Pseustes spp.).

These are just a few of the major families within the suborder Serpentes. The classification of snakes is an ongoing process, with new species being discovered. The classification of snakes provides a window into the incredible biodiversity of these remarkable reptiles, offering insights into their unique adaptations, ecology, and evolutionary history.

WHICH COUNTRY HAS THE DEADLIEST SNAKES?

🐍 Several countries are known for having some of the deadliest snakes in the world.

🐍 These venomous reptiles can pose a significant risk to humans and other animals, with their potent venom causing severe and sometimes fatal reactions.

🐍 In this section, we will discuss the countries with the highest concentration of deadly snakes and highlight some of the most dangerous species found in each region.

Australia:

🐍 Home to a wide variety of venomous snake species, including the inland taipan, the world's most venomous snake.

🐍 Other highly venomous species include the eastern brown snake, coastal taipan, and death adder.

SNAKES: AN IN-DEPTH EXPLORATION

- Despite the prevalence of venomous snakes, antivenom treatments have significantly reduced fatalities in the country.

- Papua New Guinea, just north of Australia and nearby Indonesia, also has many deadly snakes.

India:

- Known for its dangerous "Big Four" snake species: Indian cobra, Russell's viper, saw-scaled viper, and common krait.

- These four species are responsible for the majority of snakebite-related deaths in the country.

- India has the highest number of snakebite fatalities worldwide. However, many bites can be attributed to the large human population and increased interactions with snakes.

Brazil:

- Brazil is home to the highly venomous Bothrops genus, which includes species like the lancehead viper and jararaca.

- Brazil also hosts the venomous bushmaster, one of the largest pit vipers in the world.

- While snakebite fatalities are lower than in India, Brazil's diverse snake population makes it a country with a significant number of deadly species.

South Africa:

- South Africa is well-known for the infamous black mamba, one of the world's most venomous and aggressive snake species.

🐍 Other dangerous species include the puff adder, boomslang, and cape cobra.

🐍 South Africa has a lower number of snakebite fatalities compared to other countries on this list. However, the presence of these deadly species still poses a risk.

United States:

🐍 Home to several venomous snake species, primarily concentrated in the southern and western regions.

🐍 Dangerous species include the eastern and western diamondback rattlesnakes, cottonmouth, and coral snakes.

Diamondback Rattlesnake

SNAKES: AN IN-DEPTH EXPLORATION

🐍 Although fatalities are rare due to antivenom and medical care availability, these venomous snakes can still pose a significant threat.

What are the deadliest snakes in the world?

🐍 The WHO estimates that 5.4 million people are bitten by snakes each year, causing 81,000 to 138,000 fatalities.

🐍 There are various ways in which snakes kill their prey.

🐍 The production of venom and constriction are two of the most common ways snakes kill.

🐍 It is essential to know which snakes to avoid and how to stay safe in their presence.

🐍 In this section, we'll explore the world of the deadliest snakes, so buckle up and get ready to learn!

Inland Taipan:

🐍 Also known as the "fierce snake," the inland taipan is considered the deadliest snake in the world.

🐍 It can be found in Australia and has the most toxic venom of any snake.

🐍 One bite has enough venom to kill 100 men.

🐍 They strike fast and release 8 quick bites to release the venom.

🐍 The inland taipan is 1-2 meters long.

🐍 They change color with the seasons.

- They go darker in winter to absorb more sun.

- The Mulga snake is the only animal that is immune to the venom.

- The Mulga snake hunts taipans.

- The Taipan is not an aggressive snake and will only bite when threatened.

Belcher's Sea Snake:

- Found in Southeast Asia and Northern Australian waters, the belcher's sea snake is another deadly snake to be aware of.

- It has a highly toxic venom that attacks the nervous system, causing paralysis and eventually death.

- Fortunately, this snake is not known to be aggressive towards humans.

- This snake can't survive on land for very long because their scales don't allow them to move well.

Eastern Brown Snake:

- Native to Australia, the eastern brown snake is responsible for the most snakebite deaths in the country.

- It's highly venomous and can be found in both urban and rural areas.

- Its venom attacks the nervous system, causing paralysis and respiratory failure.

SNAKES: AN IN-DEPTH EXPLORATION

Black Mamba:

🐍 Found in Africa, the black mamba is one of the world's fastest and most aggressive snakes.

🐍 It's highly venomous and can deliver a lethal bite in just a few minutes. Its venom attacks the nervous system, causing paralysis and eventually death.

Tiger Snake:

🐍 Found in Australia, the Tiger Snake is highly venomous and responsible for a high number of snakebite fatalities in the country.

🐍 Its venom attacks the nervous system, causing paralysis and respiratory failure.

🐍 The tiger snake can be aggressive when threatened and should be avoided at all costs.

Philippine Cobra:

🐍 Native to the Philippines, this snake is highly venomous and can deliver a fatal bite in just a few hours.

🐍 Its venom attacks the nervous system, causing paralysis and eventually death.

🐍 The Philippine cobra is known for its ability to spit venom up to 3 meters, making it a dangerous snake to be around.

King Cobra:

🐍 Found in Southeast Asia, the king cobra is the largest venomous snake in the world.

🐍 It can deliver a deadly bite in just a few minutes, and its venom attacks the nervous system, causing paralysis and eventually death.

🐍 The king cobra is known for its aggressive behavior and should be left alone if seen.

SOME FUN FACTS ABOUT THE BLACK MAMBA

Speed Demon:

🐍 The black mamba is considered one of the fastest snakes in the world, capable of reaching speeds of up to 12 miles per hour (20 kilometers per hour), which outruns humans.

🐍 The Mamba will chase its prey and predators and easily catch them. Unless you are an Olympic runner, quickly get inside a shelter or a vehicle to protect yourself from this menace!

Size Matters:

🐍 Black mambas are among the longest venomous snakes, with adult individuals typically measuring between 8 and 14 feet (2.5 to 4.3 meters) in length. Some are even longer, making them an impressive sight in the wild.

SNAKES: AN IN-DEPTH EXPLORATION

Potent Venom:

- The black mamba's venom is highly toxic and contains powerful neurotoxins.

- A single bite from this snake can deliver enough venom to kill several adult humans quickly.

- Without urgent medical treatment, the death rate from a black mamba bite is extremely high.

Name Origin:

- Interestingly, the black mamba's name does not come from the color of its body, which is typically a shade of gray or olive green. Instead, the name refers to the inky black color of the inside of its mouth, which is revealed when the snake feels threatened and opens its mouth in a defensive display.

Lightning-Quick Strikes:

- Black mambas are known for their incredibly fast and accurate strikes.

- They can strike repeatedly in quick succession, making them a terrifying predator and a dangerous enemy when cornered.

Arboreal Lifestyle:

- Although black mambas are often found on the ground, they are also excellent climbers and can frequently be found resting in trees or bushes. This arboreal lifestyle allows them to hunt for a diverse range of prey, including birds, rodents, and other small mammals.

Shy by Nature:

🐍 Black mambas are generally shy and reclusive. They prefer to avoid confrontation with humans and other potential threats. However, if cornered or provoked, they can become aggressive and defensive, making them a dangerous encounter for the unwary.

Reproduction:

🐍 Black mambas lay eggs. A female black mamba can lay between 10 and 25 eggs in a single clutch, usually deposited in a burrow or hidden under rocks or vegetation. The eggs incubate for 2 to 3 months before the baby snakes hatch.

Distribution and Habitat:

🐍 Black mambas are native to sub-Saharan Africa, where they inhabit a range of environments, including savannas, grasslands, woodlands, and rocky areas. They are highly adaptable and can thrive in both arid and moist habitats as long as there is enough cover for them to hide and hunt.

Conservation Status:

🐍 The black mamba is currently listed as "Least Concern" on the IUCN Red List, indicating that the species is not facing any immediate threats to its survival.

Can a human outrun a black mamba?

🐍 A black mamba is one of the fastest snake species in the world, with speeds reaching up to 12-19 km/h (7-12 mph).

🐍 While this is certainly fast for a snake, an average human can reach speeds of around 10 km/h (6 mph) when running.

🐍 However, some well-trained athletes can run at speeds exceeding 20 km/h (12 mph).

🐍 Although it would be a close race, an average person might struggle to outrun a black mamba, while a trained athlete would have a better chance of doing so.

🐍 It's worth noting that black mambas are not aggressive toward humans unless threatened or cornered, so the likelihood of needing to outrun one is relatively low.

🐍 If you ever encounter a black mamba in the wild, it is best to back away slowly and give the snake space to retreat rather than attempting to outrun it. Because if you run, the black mamba will chase you.

KING COBRA: THE MAJESTIC MONARCH OF THE SNAKE WORLD

🐍 The king cobra (*Ophiophagus hannah*) is a truly remarkable creature that holds a unique place in the world of reptiles.

🐍 As the longest venomous snake on Earth, this awe-inspiring species has fascinated humans for centuries.

🐍 In this section, we will explore the king cobra's biology, behavior, and ecology, shedding light on the various aspects that make this snake a fascinating subject of study and admiration.

Physical Characteristics:

🐍 The king cobra is a large, impressive snake that can grow up to 18 feet (5.5 meters) in length. However, most individuals average around 10-13 feet (3-4 meters).

🐍 Their body is sleek and muscular, covered in smooth, overlapping scales.

🐍 The coloration of king cobras varies, ranging from olive green to brown or black, with lighter bands or chevrons adorning their bodies.

🐍 This coloration helps them blend in with their natural surroundings, providing essential camouflage so they can catch their prey.

🐍 One of the most striking features of the king cobra is its hood, which can expand when threatened or agitated.

🐍 The hood is created by elongated neck ribs that support the loose skin around the neck. When fully extended, it gives the snake an intimidating appearance.

Habitat and Distribution:

🐍 King cobras inhabit a diverse range of environments across Southeast Asia, including India, China, Indonesia, and the Philippines.

🐍 They prefer areas with dense vegetation, such as tropical rainforests, bamboo thickets, and mangrove swamps, where they can easily find shelter and hunt for prey.

SNAKES: AN IN-DEPTH EXPLORATION

- These snakes are known to be excellent climbers and swimmers, highlighting their adaptability and versatility within their chosen habitats.

- Many people remember seeing cobras dancing out of a basket in India. They are used a lot in India for entertainment. Sadly, these cobras have had their fangs removed.

Diet and Hunting Behavior:

- The king cobra is an apex predator, primarily feeding on other snakes, including venomous species like the Indian cobra and krait.

- They have also been known to prey on smaller vertebrates, such as lizards, rodents, and birds.

- When hunting, the king cobra relies on its keen senses, including its exceptional sense of smell, to locate and track its prey.

- When the king cobra meets its target prey (or predator), it delivers a swift, powerful strike, injecting its poisonous venom through its long, hollow fangs.

- The venom of a king cobra is a potent neurotoxin, causing paralysis and, ultimately, death to its prey.

- The snake will then consume its meal whole, using its flexible jaws to accommodate the size of its prey.

Reproduction and Parental Care:

🐍 King cobras exhibit unique reproductive and parental care behaviors compared to most other snake species.

🐍 Mating typically occurs during the dry season, from January to April.

🐍 The courtship process involves the male and female king cobras engaging in a ritual "dance," during which they raise their bodies and entwine around each other.

🐍 After mating, the female will seek a suitable location to build her nest. She constructs the nest using leaves, twigs, and other vegetation, creating a mound with a central chamber for her eggs.

🐍 The female can lay between 20-40 eggs, which she carefully deposits in the nest chamber.

🐍 Most snakes abandon their nest and eggs but not the female king cobra.

🐍 The female king cobra displays parental care, guarding her nest and eggs day and night against potential predators.

🐍 She will remain with her eggs until they hatch, which usually takes around 60-90 days.

🐍 After hatching, the young king cobras are left to fend for themselves as the mother departs to resume her solitary life.

CATCHING PREY

🐍 Catching prey is one of the most essential aspects of a snake's survival, and different species have developed unique ways of capturing their food.

🐍 Venomous and non-venomous snakes both have different methods of hunting and catching prey.

VENOMOUS AND NON-VENOMOUS SNAKES

🐍 **Venomous snakes** have specialized glands that produce venom, which they use to defeat and kill their prey.

🐍 They have developed complex venom delivery systems, such as hollow fangs, which allow them to inject venom into their prey.

🐍 When a venomous snake bites its prey, the venom quickly enters the bloodstream, causing paralysis or death.

🐍 Some of the most venomous snakes in the world include the inland taipan, the eastern brown snake, and the black mamba.

Inland Taipan

🐍 Venomous snakes can significantly threaten humans, pets, and livestock.

🐍 Correctly identifying venomous snakes is an important skill that can help keep you safe in the great outdoors.

Let's explore some of the most common characteristics and features that can help you distinguish between venomous and non-venomous snakes. Remember that these guidelines are general, and there may be exceptions. If you are unsure about a snake's identity, it is always best to err on the side of caution and maintain a safe distance.

HOW TO IDENTIFY VENOMOUS SNAKES

Head Shape:

🐍 One of the most noticeable differences between venomous and non-venomous snakes is the shape of their head.

🐍 Many venomous snakes have a triangular or arrow-shaped head, with a distinct "neck" region separating the head from the body.

🐍 This shape houses the large venom glands behind the snake's eyes.

🐍 In contrast, non-venomous snakes typically have a more rounded head and a less pronounced neck.

🐍 However, there are exceptions, such as the venomous coral snake, which has a rounded head.

Eye Shape:

🐍 The shape and size of a snake's eyes can also provide clues about its venomous status.

🐍 Many venomous snakes, such as vipers and pit vipers, have vertical pupils, similar to a cat's eye.

🐍 Non-venomous snakes usually have round pupils.

🐍 However, this rule does not apply to all non-venomous snakes, as the highly venomous elapid snakes, like cobras and coral snakes, have round pupils.

Scales and Patterns:

🐍 Examining a snake's scales and patterns can help you identify whether or not it is venomous.

🐍 Some venomous snakes have distinct patterns that serve as a warning to potential predators.

🐍 For example, the coral snake, which is found in the Americas, has a pattern of red, yellow, and black bands.

🐍 A helpful rhyme to remember is, "Red touches yellow, kill a fellow; red touches black, friend of Jack."

🐍 However, there are non-venomous mimics like the scarlet king snake that have similar patterns, so relying solely on coloration is not foolproof.

First aid for venomous snake bites – 8 steps (the 8 steps are bolded)

🐍 Venomous snake bites can be a serious and potentially life-threatening situation.

🐍 Knowing how to administer first aid correctly is essential to minimize the risk of severe injury or death.

🐍 This section will cover the necessary steps to take if you or someone you know has been bitten by a venomous snake.

🐍 Please remember that first aid is a temporary measure, and seeking professional medical help is always the priority.

Keep calm and reassure the victim:

🐍 Panic can worsen the situation and increase the victim's heart rate, which may lead to the venom spreading more rapidly through the body.

🐍 Encourage the person to remain as still as possible and reassure them that help is on the way.

Call for emergency medical help:

🐍 It's crucial to seek professional medical assistance as soon as possible.

🐍 Call your local emergency number and provide essential information, such as the victim's location, a description of the snake (if possible), and the symptoms they are experiencing.

🐍 If you don't have a phone, run for help.

Immobilize the affected limb:

🐍 If the bite is on an arm or leg, immobilize the affected limb using a splint or a makeshift support.

🐍 You can use a magazine and rope if that is all you have.

🐍 The goal is to keep the limb in a neutral position, roughly at the same level as the heart, to reduce blood flow and slow the spread of venom.

🐍 Avoid elevating the limb above the heart level, as this can increase venom circulation.

Remove tight clothing and jewelry:

🐍 Swelling may occur around the bite area, so remove any tight clothing or jewelry to prevent tightening and further complications.

If you have a First Aid Kit, apply a pressure immobilization bandage:

🐍 If you have a crepe or elastic bandage available, you can use the pressure immobilization technique.

🐍 Start by wrapping the bandage firmly around the bite site and then continue to wrap the entire limb, moving upwards.

🐍 The pressure should be firm but not too tight, as cutting off circulation could cause additional harm. Secure the bandage and immobilize the limb using a splint or similar support.

Monitor the victim's vital signs:

🐍 Keep an eye on the victim's breathing, pulse, and level of consciousness.

🐍 Be prepared to administer CPR if necessary, and keep emergency services updated on the victim's condition.

Do NOT attempt these actions:

🐍 There are several actions that can worsen the situation and should be avoided:

🐍 Do **NOT** attempt to suck out the venom or make incisions around the bite site. If you suck out the venom and you have a cut in your mouth or tooth, you will be affected by the poison.

- Do not apply ice or cold packs to the bite, which can cause tissue damage and restrict blood flow.

- Do not use a tourniquet, as this can cut off circulation and lead to more severe complications.

- In the past, people used tourniquets, a very tight band, to stop the poison from spreading to the body. However, the pressure quickly releases the poison into the blood when the tourniquet is released.

- Do not attempt to capture or kill the snake, as this may also put you at risk of being bitten.

- If possible, take a photo of the snake from a safe distance to help medical professionals identify the species and administer the appropriate antivenom.

- Some countries have access to universal antivenom, such as Australia, where there are many different snake bites.

Get to the hospital if the medical team can't come to you:

- Even if the victim starts to feel better, it is crucial to receive professional medical evaluation and treatment.

- The effects of venom can be delayed or worsen over time, and only a healthcare professional can provide the appropriate care and antivenom needed.

Non-venomous snakes

- Rely on other methods to capture their prey.

- Some species, such as constrictors, like pythons and boas, use their powerful bodies to suffocate their prey.

- They wrap their bodies around their prey and squeeze until the animal can no longer breathe.

- Other non-venomous snakes, like the kingsnake, are known to eat other snakes, including venomous ones. They have developed immunity to the venom of other snakes and can eat them without being harmed.

- Both venomous and non-venomous snakes have specialized senses that help them locate their prey.

- They use their eyesight to spot movement and their sense of smell to track down prey.

- Some snakes, like the rattlesnake, have a specialized organ on their face called a pit organ that allows them to detect the heat of their prey.

- This helps them locate warm-blooded animals even in the dark.

- Once a snake has caught its prey, its powerful jaws will swallow it whole.

- Snakes can unhinge their jaws, allowing them to swallow prey much larger than their own head.

- After swallowing their prey, snakes can go for weeks or even months without eating again.

SNAKE BITES TO HUMANS

🐍 Snake bites to humans can be a serious and even life-threatening issue.

🐍 While snakes usually avoid human contact, they may bite when threatened or cornered.

🐍 It's important to know what to do in case of a snake bite and how to prevent it from happening in the first place.

🐍 When a snake bites a human, the venom injected into the body can cause a range of symptoms, including pain, swelling, and even paralysis or death in severe cases.

🐍 The seriousness of the symptoms depends on several factors, such as the type of snake, the amount of venom injected, and the location of the bite.

🐍 As discussed earlier, performing First Aid and seeking medical attention immediately is crucial if you or someone you know has been bitten by a snake.

🐍 Even if the symptoms are mild, it's better to be safe than sorry and seek professional medical help.

🐍 In some cases, antivenom may be administered to counteract the effects of the venom.

🐍 Antivenom is created by injecting small amounts of snake venom into an animal, such as a horse, producing antibodies that neutralize the poison.

🐍 These antibodies are then harvested and used to create the antivenom.

🐍 In Australia, one antivenom covers all deadly snakes.

🐍 Other countries, such as India, don't have enough antivenom, so they have more deaths.

🐍 Preventing snake bites in the first place is the best course of action.

🐍 You can do this by wearing protective clothing and footwear when hiking or walking in areas where snakes are known to live.

🐍 Even a pair of jeans and boots can reduce the venom injected.

🐍 Additionally, be aware of your surroundings and avoid disturbing or provoking snakes.

WHAT DO SNAKE BITES DO TO THE HUMAN BODY?

🐍 Snake bites can have serious consequences for humans.

🐍 When a snake bites a person, its venom can quickly spread through the body and cause various symptoms.

🐍 The effects of snake bites depend on the species of snake, the amount of venom injected, and the size and health of the person bitten.

SNAKES: AN IN-DEPTH EXPLORATION

🐍 The symptoms of snake bites can range from mild to life-threatening. Common symptoms include pain, swelling, and redness at the bite site.

🐍 Some people may experience nausea, vomiting, sweating, and dizziness. In severe cases, snake bites can cause muscle weakness, difficulty breathing, and even paralysis.

🐍 Venomous snakes inject venom into their prey or predators through their fangs.

🐍 Venom can be a mixture of toxins that affect different systems in the body.

🐍 Some venom can cause blood clotting problems, while others can destroy tissues and cells.

🐍 For example, the venom of the black mamba snake contains a potent neurotoxin that affects the nervous system, leading to paralysis and respiratory failure.

🐍 On the other hand, the venom of the Russell's viper can cause tissue damage and bleeding, which can be fatal if left untreated.

🐍 In addition to seeking medical attention, there are some steps you can take to reduce the risk of snake bites.

🐍 Wear protective clothing and shoes when hiking or working in areas where snakes are known to be present.

🐍 Avoid reaching into areas where you cannot see, such as rock crevices or holes in the ground. If you encounter a snake, give it plenty of space and do not attempt to handle it.

WHAT SHOULD A HUMAN DO IF BITTEN BY A SNAKE?

🐍 If you are bitten by a snake, staying calm and acting quickly is important.

🐍 The first step is to identify the type of snake that bit you.

🐍 If you can do this safely and without putting yourself in further danger, it can help medical professionals determine the best course of treatment.

🐍 In the meantime, while waiting for medical help, you can take some steps to help slow the spread of venom.

🐍 Avoid using ice or cold compresses on the bite area, as this can actually cause further tissue damage.

🐍 It is also essential to stay hydrated and calm, as anxiety and dehydration can increase the heart rate and spread the venom more quickly through the body.

🐍 Be sure to provide medical professionals with as much information about the bite as possible, including the type of snake, if known, and the time of the bite.

HOW DO VENOMOUS SNAKES KILL THEIR PREY?

🐍 Venomous snakes have an array of unique adaptations that allow them to effectively capture and subdue their prey.

🐍 Each species of venomous snake has its own method of hunting and killing prey, but they all use some general techniques.

SNAKES: AN IN-DEPTH EXPLORATION

🐍 Venomous snakes typically use their venom to immobilize and kill their prey.

🐍 The venom is delivered through specialized fangs in the front of the snake's mouth. These fangs are hollow and connected to venom glands in the snake's head.

🐍 When a venomous snake strikes its prey, the fangs puncture the skin and inject venom into the prey's body.

🐍 The venom contains a cocktail of enzymes and toxins that quickly begin to break down the prey's tissues and organs.

🐍 The exact mechanism by which venom kills prey varies depending on the snake species.

🐍 Some venomous snakes, such as the rattlesnake, use a hemotoxic venom that attacks the victim's blood vessels and tissues, causing them to break down and bleed profusely. This can lead to rapid shock and death.

🐍 Other venomous snakes, such as the cobra, use a neurotoxic venom that attacks the victim's nervous system. This type of venom can cause paralysis, respiratory failure, and death.

🐍 Venomous snakes are also skilled hunters, using a combination of stealth, patience, and lightning-fast strikes to catch their prey.

🐍 They often wait in ambush, hiding in vegetation or other cover until prey comes within striking distance.

HOW DO NON-VENOMOUS SNAKES KILL THEIR PREY?

🐍 Studies show that around 85% of all snake species in the world are non-poisonous, i.e., completely harmless.

🐍 By being non-poisonous, it means they lack venom. You might be wondering: how do they kill their prey?

🐍 Non-venomous snakes have their own unique ways of killing their prey.

🐍 While they lack the potent venom of their venomous counterparts, they have other strategies to successfully hunt and kill their prey.

🐍 One of the most common methods used by non-venomous snakes is constriction. These snakes wrap their bodies tightly around their prey, squeezing them until they can no longer breathe.

🐍 The pressure from the constriction cuts off the prey's blood flow, ultimately leading to their death. The snake's strong muscles and specialized ribs make it possible for them to use enough force to squeeze even large prey to death.

🐍 Another method used by some non-venomous snakes is the use of glue-like saliva.

🐍 These snakes have glands in their mouths that produce a sticky saliva that helps them hold onto their prey. They then use their powerful muscles to overpower and kill the prey by crushing them.

🐍 This method is commonly used by species such as the hognose snake and the African egg-eating snake.

🐍 Some non-venomous snakes also use their teeth to kill their prey. They often have sharp, pointed teeth that they use to puncture and hold onto their prey while they wrap around and constrict them. The teeth are not used to inject venom but to hold onto the target.

🐍 Some non-venomous snakes are adapted to eating aquatic prey. For example, the common water snake has a specialized set of teeth that allows it to hold onto slippery fish and other marine animals. They also have flattened tails that serve as a rudder, helping them navigate in the water while hunting.

🐍 While we are on the subject of aquatic prey, the olive python of Australia, which is enormous, has been documented as overpowering, constricting, and eating a crocodile.

🐍 In the same way, the burmese python has been known to slide into the waters of the Everglades in Florida and swallow an alligator whole. Stay away from the waters of the Everglades I say!

🐍 Nonvenomous snakes have evolved strategies to successfully hunt and kill their prey.

🐍 While they may not have the same deadly venom as their venomous counterparts, they are still highly effective predators in their own right.

CAN A PYTHON KILL A HUMAN?

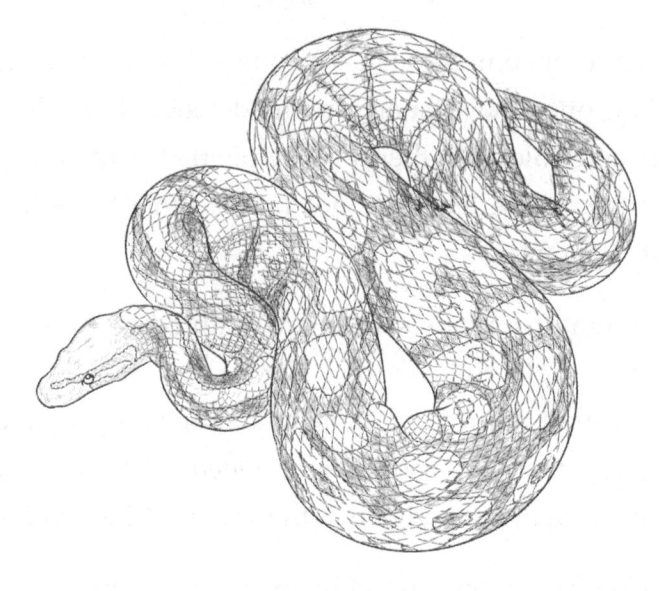

Python

🐍 Pythons are found in different parts of the world, like Africa, Asia, and Australia.

🐍 They are among the largest snakes in the world, with some species reaching lengths of up to 30 feet!

🐍 This is a whopping 9 meters for those on the metric system.

🐍 However, despite their massive size, pythons are not typically a threat to humans.

🐍 While it's true that pythons have been known to kill and even eat humans on rare occasions, these incidents are extremely rare.

🐍 As mentioned earlier, pythons are non-venomous snakes

that kill their prey by wrapping around them and squeezing until they can no longer breathe.

- Pythons are incredibly strong and can exert immense pressure on their prey.

- In fact, a python's muscles are so strong that they can crush bone!

- Most of the time, pythons in the wild will only attack humans if they feel threatened or cornered.

- For example, if a person accidentally steps on a python or tries to capture it, the snake may feel like it needs to defend itself.

- However, pythons are generally not aggressive toward humans and will avoid confrontation whenever possible.

- It's also worth noting that most pet pythons are not large enough to pose a threat to humans.

- While some species of pet pythons can grow quite large, they are typically fed a diet of mice and rats and are not aggressive toward humans.

- However, it's always important to exercise caution when handling any type of snake, including pet pythons.

- In Australia recently, an elderly lady was on the toilet when the household heard an almighty crash. Fearing she may have fallen, the family tried to enter the bathroom but could not do so by the weight of what they thought was their grandmother against the door. The ambulance and police were able to force their way in through the locked door on the other side to discover a group of enormous pythons that had crashed through the ceiling onto the floor in front of the grandmother. The grandmother fully recovered after a few days in the hospital for shock and bruising. The snake catcher was called, and the roof was fixed promptly.

WHAT TO DO IF YOU SEE A SNAKE

If you happen to come across a snake, it can be a little alarming. However, it's important to remain calm and handle the situation appropriately. Here are 5 tips on what to do if you see a snake:

1. Keep your distance: The best thing to do when you see a snake is to stay away from it. Keep a safe distance, and don't try to approach or touch it.

2. Identify the snake: If you can, try to identify the snake from a safe distance. This can help you determine if it's venomous or not. Remember, not all snakes are dangerous!

3. It's essential to **remain calm and not panic**. Most snakes won't attack unless they feel threatened or cornered. So, try to stay calm and give the snake plenty of space.

4. Back away slowly: If you can, slowly back away from the snake. Don't turn your back on it, and don't run, as this may provoke it.

5. Call for help: If the snake is venomous, or if you're not sure if it's dangerous, call for help. Contact a local wildlife expert, animal control, or emergency services for assistance.

EATING FACTS

🐍 Snakes have some unique eating habits that make them fascinating creatures to study.

🐍 For starters, snakes are carnivorous and feed on various prey depending on their species, size, and habitat.

🐍 Some species of snakes feed exclusively on rodents, while others prefer birds, amphibians, or even other snakes.

🐍 One of the most intriguing aspects of snake eating habits is their ability to swallow prey whole.

🐍 Snakes have a unique jaw structure that allows them to open their mouth wide and stretch their jaws to accommodate prey much larger than their head.

🐍 In fact, some snakes can consume prey up to twice their size! After catching their prey, snakes will begin to swallow it whole headfirst. The prey is slowly passed down the snake's long, narrow esophagus through a series of muscle contractions.

🐍 Another interesting fact about snake eating habits is their ability to go long periods without food.

🐍 Some snakes, such as the king cobra, can go months without food.

🐍 This ability to go without food is due to their slow metabolism and the fact that they can conserve energy by slowing down their bodily functions.

🐍 Snakes also have an interesting way of digesting their food.

🐍 Instead of having a stomach, snakes have a long, muscular tube called the digestive tract.

🐍 The digestive process starts in the snake's mouth, where saliva containing digestive enzymes begins to break down the prey. The prey is then slowly moved through the digestive tract, where it is further broken down, and nutrients are absorbed.

🐍 One unique aspect of snake digestion is that snakes can digest bones, fur, and feathers. This is due to the presence of powerful digestive enzymes in their stomachs that can break down almost any type of organic material.

HOW DO THEY EAT

🐍 Snakes play a vital role in our ecosystem.

🐍 They are known to help control rodent populations and other small pests, making them a tremendous environmental addition.

🐍 As pets, they can also be fantastic if given the proper environment, feeding requirements, heat, and ultraviolet lighting.

🐍 One of the most intriguing things about snakes is their food consumption.

SNAKES: AN IN-DEPTH EXPLORATION

🐍 They don't chew their food like we do, but instead, they have an impressive set of over 200 teeth that point backward toward their throats.

🐍 This helps prevent their prey from escaping. Once the target is caught, the snake will usually suffocate it by wrapping their bodies around it until it stops moving.

🐍 Then they will proceed to ingest it headfirst.

🐍 Snakes have extremely flexible lower jaws that allow them to open their mouths wide enough to consume prey that is 75-100% larger than them.

🐍 Because of this, snakes will only eat if they do not feel threatened and are in a safe place.

🐍 To prevent choking, they will push the end of their trachea (windpipe) out of their mouths, creating a snorkel effect to receive oxygen as the large prey fills their mouths.

🐍 The warmth of a snake's body plays a crucial role in the digestion process. The warmer their body, the faster they can digest their food.

🐍 Snakes typically take 3-5 days to digest a meal, but the larger the prey and the snake, the longer it takes.

🐍 Their digestive system can dissolve everything but their prey's hair, feathers, and claws, which are not entirely broken down.

🐍 If a snake feels threatened soon after eating, it will often regurgitate its food to escape.

🐍 Snakes are also known for not needing to eat very often.

🐍 They typically only need to consume 6-30 meals each year to remain healthy, depending on their age, type, and size.

🐍 This shows how efficient their bodies are at extracting nutrients from their food, making them incredible survivors in the wild.

HOW EXACTLY DO SNAKES EAT AND DIGEST?

Snakes are carnivorous and typically swallow their prey whole. Here's a brief overview of how snakes eat and digest their food:

🐍 Swallowing: Once a snake captures its prey, it will use its jaws to slowly work the quarry into its mouth. The snake's lower jaw is attached to a flexible ligament, which allows it to stretch its mouth around prey much larger than its head. The snake then uses muscular contractions to move the prey down its throat and into its stomach.

🐍 Digestion: Once the prey is in the stomach, digestive enzymes and stomach acids begin to break down the prey's flesh and organs. The digestion process is aided by the snake's unique digestive system, which includes a stretchy stomach lining and specialized muscles that help the snake to move and break down its food.

🐍 Absorption: Once the food is broken down into small particles, it is absorbed through the walls of the snake's intestines and into its bloodstream. The nutrients from the food are then used to provide the snake with energy and to help it grow and maintain its body.

🐍 Excretion: Any waste material not absorbed by the snake's body is eliminated as feces, typically expelled as a dry, white substance.

🐍 It's worth noting that the digestion process can take several days or even weeks, depending on the size of the prey and the snake's metabolism.

🐍 During this time, the snake may not eat again until the previous meal has been fully digested.

Facts about feeding captive snakes:

🐍 It is highly recommended that captive snakes be fed frozen/thawed rodents rather than live prey.

🐍 Live prey can often fight back and injure your snake, resulting in trauma, bite wounds, and potential complications due to infection.

🐍 Frozen mice and rats are bred and euthanized humanely for the consumption of snakes in captivity. They are also fed appropriate diets to ensure they are "pre-loaded" with the proper nutrients and vitamins needed for your pet's health.

🐍 Live prey may have consumed something they are not supposed to, which can result in your snake consuming something harmful.

🐍 Feeding your snake frozen/thawed rodents is also more convenient and safer for you as the owner, as you do not need to be present during the feeding process. There is no risk of injury to your snake or yourself.

HOW LONG DO SNAKES GO WITHOUT EATING?

🐍 One of the most interesting things about them is their ability to go without food for incredibly long periods.

🐍 The length of time that a snake can go without eating varies depending on its species, size, age, and availability of food in its environment.

🐍 Some species of snakes can go months without eating, while others can go over a year without a meal!

🐍 For example, the African rock python, one of the largest snakes in the world, can go up to six months without eating.

🐍 This is due to its slow metabolism and ability to conserve energy. Similarly, the king cobra can go up to six months without a meal, while the black mamba can go up to 8 months without food.

🐍 Other species of snakes, such as the garter snake, eat small meals frequently and can go only a few days without food. The snake's size also plays a role in how long it can go without eating. Smaller snakes require less food and can survive longer periods without it.

🐍 During periods of drought or food scarcity, snakes can enter a state of hibernation, where they conserve energy by slowing down their metabolism. This allows them to survive for extended periods without food.

🐍 It's important to note that even though snakes can go for long periods without eating, it doesn't mean they should.

🐍 Snakes need food to survive and thrive; long periods without eating can lead to health problems and even death.

REPRODUCTION AND LIFE CYCLE

🐍 Reproduction is a vital aspect of the life cycle of all living creatures, including lizards and snakes.

🐍 These fascinating creatures have evolved different reproductive strategies to ensure the survival of their species.

🐍 In this chapter, we will explore the reproductive strategies of snakes, including their courtship and mating behavior, egg-laying and incubation, and the growth and development of snake offspring.

🐍 Snakes use a variety of reproductive strategies to ensure their species' survival. Some species lay eggs, while others give birth to live young. In some species, females store sperm from multiple males to ensure genetic diversity in their offspring.

🐍 Courtship and mating behavior also vary among snake species.

- Some male snakes engage in elaborate courtship displays to attract females. In contrast, others rely on chemical signals to find a mate. Some species engage in combat with other males to establish dominance and gain access to females.

- Once a female snake has mated, she may lay eggs or give birth to live young.

- In egg-laying species, the female will lay her eggs in a suitable location and then leave them to incubate.

- Incubation times can vary from weeks to months, depending on the species and environmental conditions.

- In live-bearing species, the embryos develop inside the female's body, and the young are born fully formed.

- The growth and development of snake offspring can also vary significantly between species. Some hatchlings are fully independent and can fend for themselves, while others require parental care for some time.

- Some species have a high mortality rate during the early stages of development, while others have a better chance of survival.

REPRODUCTIVE STRATEGIES OF SNAKES

Snakes are some of the most intriguing creatures on Earth, with unique adaptations that have allowed them to thrive in a variety of environments. One of the most fascinating aspects of their biology is their reproductive strategies, which can vary greatly between species.

Sexual vs. Asexual Reproduction:

The majority of snake species reproduce sexually, meaning that they require a partner for fertilization to occur.

- However, some species, such as the brahminy blind snake, can reproduce asexually through a process called parthenogenesis.

- Parthenogenesis is a rare spectacle in which an unfertilized egg develops into a viable offspring.

- This ability allows the brahminy blind snake to establish populations in areas where no other snakes of their species are present, making them an impressive example of a successful reptile in the animal kingdom.

Mating Rituals:

- Snake courtship and mating rituals can be both fascinating and complex.

- Male snakes typically seek out females by following their scent trails.

- When a male finds a potential mate, he may engage in elaborate courtship behaviors to persuade her to mate. For example, in the case of garter snakes, male snakes form large "mating balls" around a single female, where multiple males compete for her attention.

SNAKES: AN IN-DEPTH EXPLORATION

🐍 This display can be quite a sight to behold and is a clear example of the lengths some snake species will go to secure a mate.

🐍 More about this in the next chapter.

Oviparous, Ovoviviparous, and Viviparous:

Snakes employ various strategies to bring their offspring into the world. There are three primary reproductive methods: oviparous, ovoviviparous, and viviparous. Let's explore each one in more detail:

1. Oviparous:

🐍 This is the most common reproductive strategy among snakes, with around 70% of species laying eggs.

🐍 Oviparous snakes, such as the ball python and king cobra, will deposit their eggs in a protected location, like a burrow or under a log.

🐍 The mother often leaves the eggs to incubate on their own. However, some species, like the python, are known to coil around their eggs to maintain temperature and protect them from predators.

2. Ovoviviparous:

🐍 This method involves eggs being retained within the female's body during development.

🐍 The eggs have a thin, permeable shell, allowing the developing embryos to receive nutrients and oxygen from the mother.

🐍 Once the eggs are ready to hatch, the mother gives birth to live young. Examples of ovoviviparous snakes include the boa constrictor and the rattlesnake.

3. Viviparous:

🐍 In viviparous snakes, the embryos develop within the mother's body and receive nutrients and oxygen through a placenta-like structure.

🐍 This method is relatively rare in snakes, with only a small number of species, such as the green anaconda, employing this reproductive strategy.

🐍 Viviparous snakes give birth to live young, which are typically more developed and independent than those born through oviparity or ovoviviparity.

🐍 Often the live young simply swim away or slither away and are ready to be independent.

Brood Care:

🐍 While many snake species provide little or no parental care after giving birth, some exceptions exist.

🐍 For instance, the king cobra, which is the world's longest venomous snake, is known for its impressive parental care.

🐍 The female builds a nest from leaves and vegetation, where she lays her eggs.

COURTSHIP AND MATING BEHAVIOR

🐍 Snakes exhibit a fascinating array of courtship and mating behaviors that are crucial to their reproductive success.

🐍 These behaviors are often complex and can vary significantly between species.

🐍 In this section, we will delve deeper into the world of snake courtship and mating, providing a comprehensive overview of the various strategies and rituals that different snake species use to ensure the continuation of their lineage.

Pheromones and Scent Trails:

🐍 Communication is key to snakes' courtship and mating process, with pheromones playing a central role.

🐍 Female snakes release chemical signals called pheromones, which can be detected by male snakes through their Jacobson's organs.

🐍 The male will follow the female scent.

Courtship Displays:

🐍 Once a male snake has located a female, he must convince her to mate.

🐍 Courtship displays are essential to this process, and different snake species have unique rituals.

🐍 Some common courtship behaviors include:

🐍 Body Rubbing: The male snake may rub his body along the female's to stimulate her and demonstrate his interest in mating. This rubbing can also help spread his pheromones onto the female, making her more receptive to his advances.

🐍 Wrestling: In some snake species, such as rattlesnakes and garter snakes, males engage in wrestling matches to establish dominance and win the right to mate with a female. These bouts can be intense, with males coiling around each other, attempting to pin their opponent to the ground. The winner gets to court and mate with the female, while the loser must search for another mate.

🐍 The "Dance of Love": In certain species, such as the adder or the cottonmouth, the courtship ritual may resemble a dance. The male and female snake entwines their bodies and raises their heads off the ground, sometimes swaying back and forth in a mesmerizing display.

🐍 Mating Balls: As mentioned earlier, some snakes, like garter snakes, form large "mating balls" where numerous males congregate around a single female. The males compete for the female's attention, with the most persistent and successful male getting the opportunity to mate.

Post-Mating Behavior

🐍 After mating, the male and female snakes typically go their separate ways.

🐍 However, in some species, the male may continue to court and mate with other females, while the female focuses on finding a suitable location to lay her eggs or give birth.

EGG-LAYING AND INCUBATION IN SNAKES

🐍 Snakes that lay eggs, known as oviparous snakes, comprise around 70% of all snake species.

🐍 Egg-laying and incubation are crucial aspects of their reproductive strategy, ensuring the survival and success of their offspring.

🐍 In this section, we will explore the fascinating process of egg-laying and incubation in snakes, discussing the various steps and factors contributing to successfully hatching these reptilian embryos.

EGG-LAYING PROCESS:

🐍 Once a female snake has successfully mated and fertilized her eggs, she will begin the process of egg-laying, or oviposition.

🐍 The time between mating and egg-laying can vary greatly depending on the species, ranging from a few weeks to several months.

🐍 Before laying her eggs, the female snake will search for a suitable location that provides the necessary conditions for successful incubation.

🐍 This can include factors such as temperature, humidity, and protection from predators. Common nesting sites include burrows, crevices, or beneath logs and vegetation.

🐍 The female snake will lay her eggs once the perfect site has been found.

🐍 The number of eggs laid can vary widely between species and even within the same species, depending on factors such as the size and age of the female.

🐍 For example, a corn snake may lay between 10 and 30 eggs, while a large python could lay over 100 eggs in a single clutch.

EGG STRUCTURE AND COMPOSITION:

🐍 Snake eggs are different from the familiar bird eggs in several ways.

🐍 The shell of a snake egg is not hard but somewhat leathery and pliable, allowing for gas exchange during incubation.

🐍 This soft shell also expands the egg as the developing embryo grows inside.

🐍 Inside the egg, the embryo is surrounded by a liquid called the amniotic fluid, which provides cushioning and protection. Additionally, the egg contains a yolk sac, which supplies the developing snake with the necessary nutrients for growth.

INCUBATION:

🐍 Incubation is the period between egg-laying and hatching when the developing embryos rely on environmental conditions to successfully mature.

🐍 The temperature and humidity within the nesting site play a crucial role in incubation. If it's too cold, some male snakes, such as the King Cobra, will sit on the eggs.

🐍 For most snake species, the ideal incubation temperature ranges between 78°F and 90°F (25°C to 32°C), with humidity levels around 70% to 90%.

🐍 Variations from these conditions can lead to developmental issues, delayed hatching, or even the death of the embryos.

🐍 The incubation period varies from 45 to 75 days.

🐍 Some species, such as the African rock python, may have an incubation period of up to 90 days or more.

PARENTAL CARE DURING INCUBATION:

🐍 The degree of parental care during incubation varies between snake species.

🐍 Many snakes, like the majority of colubrid, provide little or no parental care after laying their eggs, leaving the eggs to incubate on their own.

🐍 Some species, such as pythons, display exceptional maternal care.

🐍 The female python will coil around her clutch of eggs, protecting them from predators and maintaining the optimal temperature for incubation.

🐍 She achieves this by contracting her muscles, generating heat through a process called shivering thermogenesis.

🐍 The female python will also adjust her coils to regulate humidity, ensuring the eggs are not too dry or moist.

HIBERNATION

🐍 You might be wondering if snakes do hibernate. Yes, they do.

🐍 Many people assume that snakes are active all year round. Still, in fact, they do hibernate just like many other animals.

🐍 During hibernation, snakes enter dormancy, where their metabolic rate decreases significantly, allowing them to conserve energy.

🐍 This is usually triggered by changes in temperature and daylight hours. In colder regions, snakes may hibernate for months during the winter. In contrast, in warmer areas, they may hibernate for shorter periods or not at all.

🐍 When snakes hibernate, they seek out underground shelters where the temperature is more stable and can avoid freezing temperatures.

SNAKES: AN IN-DEPTH EXPLORATION

🐍 This can include burrows, crevices, or even human-made structures like basements or tunnels. Some species may hibernate in large groups to conserve and share body heat.

🐍 During hibernation, snakes may appear lifeless, and their breathing may become slow and shallow.

🐍 They may also become more vulnerable to predators, which is why they look for secure hiding places.

🐍 However, they are still alive, and their body systems continue to function, but at a much slower rate.

🐍 It's important to note that not all snakes hibernate, and some species may go through a period of inactivity instead.

🐍 For example, in hotter regions, some snakes may enter a state of torpor during the hottest part of the year, reducing their activity and metabolism to conserve water.

🐍 Understanding hibernation in snakes can give us a greater appreciation for these incredible animals and their unique adaptations to survive in different environments.

🐍 It also highlights the importance of preserving habitats and protecting snakes from disturbance during this vulnerable time.

MORE SNAKEY FACTS

Animals that snakes are scared of:

🐍 Snakes have many predators in the wild, including birds of prey, larger snakes, and some mammals such as coyotes and foxes.

🐍 However, some animals are natural enemies of snakes, which can be helpful to know if you encounter a snake in the wild.

🐍 For example, some species of mongoose are well known for their ability to kill venomous snakes, while certain types of birds, such as the secretary bird, are known to stomp on snakes to kill them.

🐍 Some species of frogs, lizards, and even other snakes are also known to eat snakes.

Antivenom:

🐍 Antivenom, also known as **antivenin or antivenom serum**, is a medication made from animal antibodies that is used to treat venomous snakebites.

🐍 The antivenom is created by injecting a small amount of venom from a specific species of snake into an animal, such as a horse, and then harvesting the antibodies produced by the animal's immune system in response to the venom.

🐍 When administered to a person who has been bitten by a venomous snake, the antivenom works by binding to the venom in the person's bloodstream and neutralizing its harmful effects.

🐍 The antibodies in the antivenom essentially act as an antidote to the venom, preventing it from causing further damage to the person's body.

🐍 It's important to note that antivenom is species-specific, meaning that it is only effective against the venom from the specific species of snake for which it was created.

🐍 For this reason, it's important to identify the snake species responsible for the bite to administer the appropriate antivenom.

🐍 In many developed countries, one antivenom is used for all snake bites.

🐍 While snakes can be dangerous to humans, it is essential to remember that they are usually more afraid of us than we are of them.

Snakes camouflage to protect themselves:

🐍 Many species of snakes are well adapted to blending in with their surroundings, which helps them stay hidden from predators and avoid detection by prey.

🐍 Some snakes, like the green tree python, have bright, vibrant colors that allow them to blend in with foliage and other vegetation.

🐍 Others, like the diamondback rattlesnake, have patterns that mimic the color and texture of rocks and other natural features.

🐍 Some species of snakes can also change color to match their surroundings, which can help them avoid detection.

Huff, puff, hiss, rattle the tail:

🐍 When threatened, many species of snakes will use a variety of defensive behaviors to protect themselves.

🐍 Some, like the cobra, will puff up their bodies and hiss loudly to try to intimidate their attacker.

🐍 Others, like rattlesnakes, will rattle their tails to warn potential predators of their presence.

🐍 Some species, like the hognose snake, will even play dead or feign injury to avoid attack.

🐍 It is important to remember that if you encounter a snake in the wild, the best course of action is to give it plenty of space and avoid provoking it in any way.

FAMOUS SNAKE STORIES

🐍 Snakes have been a part of human culture and mythology for thousands of years, and many famous snake stories have been passed down through the ages.

🐍 Some of these stories are based on actual events, while others are purely fictional. Still, they all have one thing in common: they capture the imagination and keep us enthralled.

THE CLEOPATRA INCIDENT

🐍 According to ancient Roman-era writers such as Strabo, Plutarch, and Cassius Dio, Cleopatra poisoned herself using either a toxic ointment or by introducing the poison with a sharp implement, such as a hairpin.

🐍 Some historians hypothesize that Cleopatra's Roman political rival, Octavian, forced her to kill herself.

🐍 Popular belief suggests that Cleopatra committed suicide by allowing an asp (Egyptian cobra) to bite her, but the validity of ancient reports involving snakebites as the cause of death is disputed.

🐍 Additionally, it is unknown whether Cleopatra was murdered or not.

🐍 Cleopatra's death has been depicted in various works of art throughout history, ranging from sculptures and paintings to poetry and plays, as well as modern films. Ancient Greco-Roman sculptures such as the Esquiline Venus and Sleeping Ariadne served as inspirations for later artworks portraying her death, universally involving the snakebite of an asp.

THE OPHIDIOPHOBIA INCIDENT

🐍 Ophidiophobia, or the fear of snakes, is a common phobia affecting many people worldwide. For some, the fear is mild and can be easily overcome. Still, it can be debilitating for others and interfere with daily life.

🐍 The Ophidiophobia Incident is a famous case in which the fear of snakes significantly impacted a person's life.

🐍 In 2001, a woman in Florida filed a lawsuit against a theme park after she was attacked by a Burmese python during a live snake show.

🐍 The incident sparked a debate about the safety of handling snakes in public settings. It led to increased regulation of exotic animal shows.

SNAKE ISLAND

🐍 Ilha da Queimada Grande, or Snake Island, is an uninhabited island off Brazil's coast home to thousands of venomous golden lancehead snakes.

🐍 The island is considered one of the most dangerous places in the world due to the high density of snakes and is off-limits to the public.

🐍 It's related to the Fer-de-lance, the deadliest snake in the Americas.

THE MEDUSA INCIDENT

🐍 In 2018, a South Carolina woman made headlines after being bitten by a copperhead snake while shopping in a garden center.

🐍 The bite caused her hand to swell and turn purple, and she required hospitalization and antivenom treatment to recover.

THE SOUTH AFRICAN INCIDENT

🐍 More recently, in 2023, a pilot of a small Cessna was coming in to land with 4 passengers.

🐍 He could feel what he thought was his water bottle up against his legs.

🐍 As he approached to land, he saw that it wasn't a water bottle at all!

🐍 It was a Cape King Cobra. He froze and radioed the situation to the traffic control tower.

🐍 The pilot informed the passengers as the cobra then went from the legs of the pilot, up to his shirt and under his shirt.

🐍 At the last minute, the cobra slithered back under the pilot's seat, and the pilot just concentrated on landing.

🐍 The cobra disembarked at the next airport!

THE AUSTRALIAN INCIDENT

🐍 At the beginning of 2023, a male tourist north of Cairns in Queensland was admiring a python in a tree in the rainforest.

🐍 He stayed there a while, videoing the snake and getting a bit too close.

🐍 At lightning speed, the snake struck out and bit the man on his head and face, causing excessive bleeding. The teeth were sharp but without venom; the man quickly recovered.

🐍 This goes back to the warning about leaving snakes alone.

FAMOUS SNAKE HANDLERS

George H. W. Bush

🐍 One of the most famous snake handlers in the world was a Pentecostal pastor named George H. W. Bush (not to be confused with the previous President of the United States.)

🐍 He was known as "The Snake-Handling Preacher." He gained fame for his controversial practice of handling venomous snakes during his church services.

🐍 Bush's snake-handling practice was based on a literal interpretation of the Bible, specifically Mark 16:18, which says, "They will pick up serpents with their hands; and if they drink any deadly poison, it will not hurt them; they will lay their hands on the sick, and they will recover."

🐍 Bush believed that handling venomous snakes was a test of faith and a way to demonstrate God's protection.

🐍 Bush's practice was controversial and dangerous, as several of his followers were bitten by snakes, and some died from their injuries.

🐍 In 2012, Bush himself died from a snake bite during a church service in West Virginia.

🐍 While Bush's practice of snake handling is not widely accepted or condoned by mainstream religious organizations, he remains a significant figure in the history of religious snake handling in the United States.

Jackie Bibby

🐍 Jackie Bibby, also known as "The Texas Snake Man," is a famous snake handler who gained notoriety for his dangerous stunts involving venomous snakes.

🐍 Bibby was born on July 31, 1958, in Hamlin, Texas, and grew up catching snakes as a hobby.

🐍 He later turned his passion into a profession and became a snake handler, traveling the country and performing in shows and exhibitions.

🐍 Bibby is best known for setting multiple world records for his feats with snakes.

🐍 In 2005, he set the world record for holding the most rattlesnakes in his mouth, with a total of 13 snakes.

🐍 He later broke his own record in 2009, holding 11 rattlesnakes and a tarantula in his mouth for a total of 10 seconds.

🐍 Bibby has also set records for holding the most rattlesnakes with his bare hands and staying in a bathtub filled with the most rattlesnakes.

🐍 Bibby's passion for snakes has not been without its dangers. He has been bitten by venomous snakes, including rattlesnakes, copperheads, and cottonmouths numerous times.

🐍 In 2012, he suffered a severe snake bite during a performance and was rushed to the hospital in critical condition.

SNAKES: AN IN-DEPTH EXPLORATION

🐍 Despite the risks, Bibby continues to handle snakes and share his knowledge and love for these creatures with the public. He has appeared in various documentaries and TV shows, including Animal Planet's "Rattlesnake Republic" and Discovery Channel's "Venom Hunters."

🐍 Bibby is not without controversy, as some argue that his stunts with venomous snakes are dangerous and unnecessary. However, he maintains that his work is important for raising awareness about snakes and dispelling myths and fears about them.

🐍 In addition to his work as a snake handler, Bibby is also involved in wildlife conservation efforts and runs his own wildlife sanctuary in Texas. He is a respected expert in the field of herpetology. He continues to inspire and educate others with his passion for snakes.

The Irula tribe

🐍 The Irula tribe is an indigenous community that has lived in India for centuries.

🐍 One of their traditional occupations is snake handling, which they have used for snake hunting and removal.

🐍 The Irula people have developed a reputation for their exceptional skill in handling snakes and have become famous for their unique techniques.

🐍 The Irula tribe is known for its ability to track snakes and other reptiles, using their extensive knowledge of the land and natural environment to locate and catch them.

- The Irula people are adept at handling venomous snakes, such as cobras and vipers. They are also skilled at identifying different species of snakes and their behaviors.

- In recent years, the Irula tribe has gained international recognition for its snake-handling expertise.

- They have been hired by zoos and wildlife parks around the world to capture and relocate snakes that are causing problems and have even been called upon to assist in scientific research on snakes.

- One famous Irula snake handler is Vava Suresh, who has caught more than 30,000 snakes throughout his career.

- Suresh is known for his fearless approach to handling snakes and is widely regarded as one of the best snake handlers in India.

- Another well-known Irula snake handler is Rajasekharan Parameswaran, who has also gained a reputation for his expert snake-handling skills.

- Parameswaran has been featured in numerous documentaries and television shows, showcasing his unique ability to capture and relocate snakes.

- Despite their fame, the Irula tribe faces many challenges, including losing their traditional hunting grounds and the encroachment of urbanization on their land.

- However, their traditional knowledge and skills in snake handling continue to be passed down from generation to generation, ensuring that this ancient tradition remains alive and well.

Barry Goldsmith

🐍 Barry Goldsmith is a well-known Australian snake handler and wildlife educator.

🐍 He has worked with snakes for over 30 years. He has gained a reputation for his expertise and dedication to reptile conservation.

🐍 Goldsmith is particularly known for his work with venomous snakes and is often called upon to remove dangerous snakes from residential areas.

🐍 Goldsmith is the owner and operator of Snake Catcher Victoria. This business provides snake removal services and wildlife education programs to the local community.

🐍 He has appeared on numerous television programs and news segments to discuss snake safety and provide expert advice on handling and identifying snakes.

🐍 Goldsmith is also actively involved in the conservation of reptiles and regularly participates in research projects and surveys to monitor snake populations.

🐍 In addition to his work as a snake handler, Goldsmith is also a passionate educator and regularly speaks at schools and community events about the importance of snake conservation and safety.

🐍 He has also authored several books on snakes and reptiles, including "The Snake Book: The Comprehensive Guide to Snake Care and Use" and "Australian Snakes: A Natural History."

Simon Keys and Siouxsie Gillett

🐍 Simon Keys and Siouxsie Gillett are a famous husband and wife team of snake handlers and wildlife experts based in South Africa.

🐍 They have gained worldwide recognition for their work on the National Geographic channel show "Snake City," which documents their daily work of capturing and relocating dangerous snakes in urban and rural areas.

🐍 Born and raised in England, Simon Keys has been handling snakes since age eight.

🐍 His passion for reptiles eventually led him to South Africa, where he worked in the film industry before starting his own reptile removal company.

🐍 Siouxsie Gillett, born in South Africa, grew up on a game reserve and developed a love for wildlife at a young age.

🐍 She later worked as a safari guide before joining Simon in his snake removal business.

🐍 Together, Simon and Siouxsie have over 50 years of experience handling and relocating snakes.

🐍 They specialize in removing venomous snakes from homes and businesses and rescuing and rehabilitating injured snakes.

SNAKES: AN IN-DEPTH EXPLORATION

🐍 Their approach to snake handling is unique. They use minimal force and stress on the snakes, which they believe is vital to a successful relocation.

🐍 Aside from their work on "Snake City," Simon and Siouxsie are also active in educating the public about snake safety and conservation.

🐍 They often speak at schools and events, emphasizing the importance of coexisting with snakes in their natural habitats.

🐍 Simon and Siouxsie's expertise and passion for snakes have earned them a large following of fans and admirers worldwide.

🐍 Their work has helped protect people from dangerous snake encounters and promotes respect and appreciation for these often-misunderstood creatures.

Steve Irwin, "The Crocodile Hunter"

🐍 Steve Irwin, also known as "The Crocodile Hunter," was an Australian wildlife expert and television personality who gained worldwide fame for his fearless and passionate approach to handling dangerous animals.

🐍 Although he was known for his work with crocodiles, he also had experience handling snakes and other reptiles.

🐍 Irwin's love for animals began at a young age when he worked at his family's reptile park in Queensland, Australia.

🐍 He gained a deep understanding and respect for animals, especially reptiles, which he believed were often misunderstood and mistreated.

🐍 In 1991, he took over the park. He renamed it the Australia Zoo, where he continued to promote conservation and education about wildlife.

🐍 Irwin's popularity skyrocketed in the late 1990s and early 2000s with the debut of his television series "The Crocodile Hunter" on Animal Planet.

🐍 The show featured Irwin and his wife, Terri, traveling the world to educate viewers about different species of animals and their habitats.

🐍 His enthusiastic and daring approach to handling animals, including snakes, captivated audiences and made him a household name.

🐍 Irwin was known for his expertise in handling a variety of snakes, including venomous species such as the king cobra and black mamba.

Black Mamba

🐍 He had a deep respect for these animals and believed that they were often feared and persecuted unnecessarily.

🐍 He often used his platform to educate viewers about the importance of snakes in their ecosystems and the dangers of misunderstanding and mistreating them.

🐍 Tragically, Irwin died in 2006 at the age of 44 after being pierced in the chest by a stingray's barb while filming a documentary.

🐍 His death shocked his fans and the wildlife community. Still, his legacy lives on through his work and the continued efforts of the Australia Zoo to promote conservation and education about wildlife.

🐍 In addition to Irwin, there have been many other famous snake handlers throughout history, including Bill Haast, who owned the Miami Serpentarium and was known for his work with venomous snakes, and Ernie Kovacs, a comedian and television personality who was known for his love of snakes and often featured them in his comedy sketches.

WILD EXTRA RANDOM FACTS ABOUT SNAKES' BODIES

🐍 Unlike most animals, snakes do not have eyelids.

🐍 They have a protective layer over their eyes that they shed every time they shed their skin.

🐍 If you see a snake, it will be staring at you as it cannot blink.

🐍 Speaking of eyes, most snakes are blind. So if you think they are making eye contact, don't worry; they aren't.

🐍 Snakes see only red and green blurry colors.

🐍 Polycephaly is a rare condition in reptiles and mammals, where the animal has two or more heads.

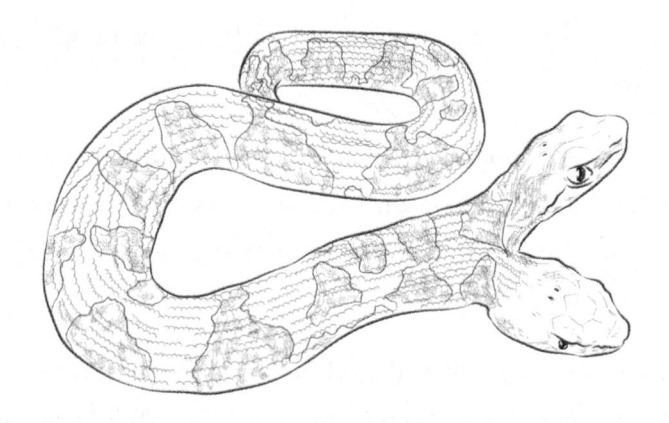

Two-Headed Snake

🐍 Snakes have the highest occurrence in the world per species, having two or more heads on one body.

🐍 Sometimes the heads of a multi-headed snake will fight each other for food. In fact, some snakes with more than one head eat the other head(s)!

🐍 Back to the head, sometimes people kill a snake out of fear and cut off their head. The snake's body can still move due to the nerve endings. Interestingly, the decapitated snake can still bite for many hours and is still quite venomous.

🐍 They smell with their tongues: Snakes use their tongues to pick up scent particles from the air and ground, which they then process using a specialized organ in their mouth called the Jacobson's organ.

🐍 They have flexible jaws: Snakes have jaws that are not attached to their skull, allowing them to swallow prey much larger than their head.

🐍 They have no ears: Snakes do not have external ears like humans and many other animals. Instead, they pick up sound vibrations through their jawbone and inner ear.

🐍 Some snakes can fly: Yes, you read that right! The Paradise Tree Snake, found in Southeast Asia, can glide through the air for distances of up to 100 meters by flattening its body and rippling in the air.

🐍 In some parts of Asia, like Borneo, there are a species of flying snakes. These snakes can glide over 330 ft (100m).

🐍 They have heat-sensing pits: Some snakes, such as the pit viper, have specialized pits on their heads that can detect infrared radiation, allowing them to locate prey in the dark.

🐍 Snakes can shed their skin: As snakes grow, they shed their skin periodically in a process called ecdysis. The old skin splits and the snake wriggles out of it, revealing shiny new skin underneath.

🐍 They don't have legs: Unlike most animals, snakes do not have legs. Instead, they move by slithering along the ground using their muscular bodies and scales.

- They have sharp, curved teeth: Snakes have teeth that are curved backward to help them grasp and hold onto prey.

- Snakes have scales: Their scales protect them from injury and help them to move smoothly on rough surfaces.

- They can swim: Many snakes are good swimmers and can easily move through the water.

- Some snakes can change color: Some species of snakes can change the color of their skin to blend in with their surroundings or to communicate with other snakes.

- They can sense vibrations: Snakes can pick up vibrations through the ground with their sensitive skin, allowing them to detect nearby prey or predators.

- Snakes can dislocate their jaws: To swallow prey larger than their head, snakes can dislocate their jaws and move the bones in their skull.

- Snakes have long, flexible bodies: The shape of a snake's body allows them to move easily through tight spaces and wrap around objects to hold on.

- They can go long periods without food: Depending on the species, snakes can go several weeks, months, or even years without eating.

- If a snake eats prey that is far too big, such as a deer, the snake can actually explode and die.

- Albino snakes are sensitive to the sun, which is an issue when they need it to survive.

SNAKES: AN IN-DEPTH EXPLORATION

- Most snakes sleep 16 hours per day.

- A venomous snake can kill itself by biting itself and the venom going directly into the bloodstream.

- Venomous snakes kill about 90 000 people a year around the world.

- This seems like a lot, but more than 1 million people die from mosquitoes every year globally.

- Native to the Amazon rainforests in South America, the green anaconda is seen to be the heaviest snake in the world. It is approximately 500 lb (230kg) in weight and about 30 ft (9m) in length.

- The inland taipan of Australia is so lethal that one venom extraction could kill 100 men.

- One in three humans, that is 30%, have a phobia of snakes.

- Snakes drink with their throats.

- They put their lower jaw in the water and vacuum it out directly into their throats to drink.

- Snakes never stop growing.

- A stressed snake can eat itself.

- Half of all snake bites in the world come from India.

- Sea snakes are so flat that they can't travel on land.

🐍 However, land snakes can travel across the water quickly to escape predators. They can hide underwater for quite a long time as well.

🐍 Snakes swallow their food whole because they can't chew. Even small foods.

🐍 A snake's fangs only last about 6 weeks or longer – depending on how often they are used for biting.

🐍 A snake will then grow more fangs.

🐍 Snakes can get head colds.

🐍 The king cobra is very shy but is also one of the most intelligent snakes.

🐍 The Mozambique cobra has a very accurate spitting rate of 100%.

🐍 The rattlesnake's tail rattle muscle is in the top 1% fastest moving muscles in all animals.

🐍 Non-venomous newborn snakes can have as much venom as an adult snake – so don't try to pet one.

CONCLUSION

Throughout this book, you have embarked on an exciting journey through the world of snakes. Whether you like snakes or fear them, there is no denying how fascinating they are. In this book, we have uncovered where snakes live, the differences between venomous and non-venomous snakes, and their sizes and shapes. We have also looked at some particular snakes, like the king Cobra, the rattlesnake, and the black mamba. We have discussed many random wild facts about snakes. They are an incredible mystery; whichever you feel about a snake, you should always know what to do if you see a snake and what first aid you should apply to yourself or a friend while looking for help.

In summary, the key to managing a venomous snake bite is to remain calm, immobilize the affected area, and seek professional medical help immediately. Proper first aid can significantly improve the victim's chances of a full recovery. Still, following the recommended steps and avoiding potentially harmful actions is essential.

Now that we have gone through the slithery world of snakes, it's time to venture into the sun-baking world of lizards.

LIZARDS: AN IN-DEPTH EXPLORATION

Frilled neck lizard

INTRODUCTION

Lizards have existed for millions of years. They have been around since the Fossil Period, which was well over 200 million years ago. Lizards are a diverse group of reptiles, with over 6000 species. They are found in almost all parts of the world, from Australia's deserts to Brazil's rainforests, ranging from tiny chameleons to large komodo dragons that can grow longer than 10 feet. Lizards are truly amazing animals that have adapted to survive in some of the harshest environments on the planet.

In this book, we'll take a journey through the world of lizards. We will explore the different types of lizards, examine their physiology, as well as share some wild facts about their bodies. We will look at the incredible adaptations that make them successful in catching prey and hiding from predators.

We'll also delve into the eating habits of lizards, including how they eat and how long they can go without food. We'll explore what predators they have in the wild. We'll also discuss how they protect themselves, from camouflaging to losing their tails.

Finally, we'll share some famous lizard news stories from around the world.

Let's step through the fascinating world of lizards.

WHAT'S A LIZARD?

🦎 Lizards are reptiles and part of the animal kingdom.

🦎 They belong to the order Squamata, which also includes snakes.

🦎 There are over 6,000 species of lizards found worldwide.

🦎 Lizards have scales covering their bodies, which are made of keratin (the same as human skin and hair).

🦎 They are cold-blooded, meaning their body temperature depends on the sun for energy and the shade when it's too hot.

🦎 Most lizards have four legs, clutched feet, and a long tail.

🦎 Some species, like legless lizards, have no limbs.

🦎 Lizards have a tail, which can be detached in some species to escape predators.

🦎 They generally have small heads and short necks.

🦎 Many lizards lay eggs, but some species give live birth.

🦎 Some well-known lizard species include geckos, chameleons, iguanas, and monitor lizards.

🦎 Lizards have various adaptations for their environments, like camouflage, color-changing abilities, or strong gripping feet for climbing. We will look more into that later in the book.

GENERAL FACTS ABOUT LIZARDS

Classification:

🦎 Belong to the reptile class

🦎 Part of the suborder "Lacertilia"

🦎 Over 6,000 species worldwide

Physical characteristics:

🦎 Cold-blooded animals

🦎 Dry, scaly skin

🦎 Most have four legs and a long tail

🦎 Some can detach and regrow their tail

🦎 Eye movement: independently moving eyes

LIZARDS: AN IN-DEPTH EXPLORATION

Habitats:

🦎 Found on all continents except Antarctica

🦎 Prefer warm climates

🦎 Live in deserts, forests, grasslands, and wetlands

Diet:

🦎 Mostly carnivorous

🦎 Insects, spiders, and small animals

🦎 Some species are vegetarians

Reproduction:

🦎 Most lay eggs (oviparous)

🦎 Some give live birth (viviparous)

🦎 Mating rituals include displays of color and physical posturing

Notable species:

🦎 Komodo dragon: largest living lizard, native to Indonesia

🦎 Chameleon: color-changing ability, lives in Africa and Madagascar

🦎 Gecko: adhesive toe pads found in warm climates worldwide

🦎 Iguana: herbivorous, located in Central and South America

Iguana

🦎 Gila monster: venomous, native to the southwestern United States and Mexico

Fun facts:

🦎 Some lizards can run on water (basilisk lizard).

🦎 The flying gecko can glide from tree to tree.

🦎 Some lizards can change their appearance to look like a dangerous predator (Mimicry.)

🦎 Lizards can live as long as 50 years.

🦎 Some lizards squirt blood out of their eyes to scare predators away.

🦎 Most lizards can swim.

🦎 Some lizards never drink water in their life.

LIZARDS: AN IN-DEPTH EXPLORATION

🦎 Baby lizards are called hatchlings.

🦎 Some lizards have two heads! The bearded dragon does produce lizards with two heads, but they usually have health problems and die young.

BEHAVIOR OF LIZARDS

Living in Groups:

🦎 Some lizard species are solitary, while many live in groups.

🦎 Examples of social lizards include green iguanas and some species of spiny-tailed lizards.

🦎 Solitary lizards, like geckos, interact with other lizards primarily during the breeding season.

Sleeping Habits:

🦎 Lizards do sleep, but their sleep patterns can vary.

🦎 Diurnal lizards, like the green anole, are active during the day and sleep at night.

🦎 Nocturnal lizards, like geckos, are active at night and sleep during the day.

LIZARDS: AN IN-DEPTH EXPLORATION

🦎 Lizards have eyelids, which they close while sleeping to protect their eyes.

Other Behaviors:

🦎 Lizards communicate using their body posture, with color changes, and by head-bobbing.

🦎 They can regulate their body temperature by basking in the sun or seeking shade.

🦎 Lizards shed their skin regularly, allowing for growth and maintaining skin health.

🦎 Some species, like the chameleon, can change their skin color for camouflage or communication.

🦎 Many lizards can lose or drop their tails to escape predators; the tail later grows back.

🦎 Lizards have a variety of diets, ranging from insects and small animals to fruits and flowers.

Feeding Habits:

🦎 Lizards have different feeding habits depending on their species.

🦎 Insectivorous lizards, like geckos and anoles, mostly eat insects and spiders.

🦎 Herbivorous lizards, like the green iguana, consume leaves, fruits, and flowers.

🦎 Omnivorous lizards, like the bearded dragon, eat both plant and animal matter.

🦎 Some lizards, like the komodo dragon, are apex predators and can take down large prey (more about the komodos later)!

Locomotion:

🦎 Lizards have different moving methods, depending on their environment and body structure.

🦎 Most lizards walk or run on four legs, using a sprawling or semi-sprawling posture – like their back legs are crawling.

🦎 Geckos have specialized toe pads that allow them to climb vertical surfaces and even walk on ceilings.

🦎 Chameleons have zygodactylous feet, which help them grip branches and navigate through trees.

🦎 What are zygodactylous feet? This means two of their toes are directed backward, and the other two point forward.

🦎 Some lizards, like the frilled-neck lizard, can run on their back legs to escape predators.

Reproduction:

🦎 Lizards reproduce either by laying eggs (oviparous) or giving birth to live young (viviparous).

🦎 Oviparous lizards lay eggs in a safe location, such as a tunnel or a crevice.

LIZARDS: AN IN-DEPTH EXPLORATION

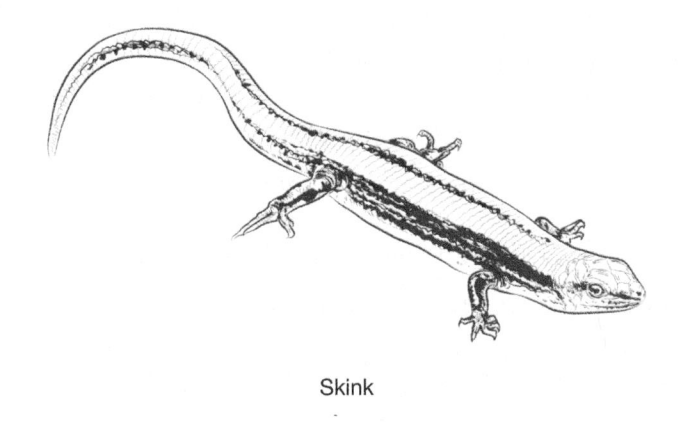

Skink

🦎 Viviparous lizards, like the blue-tailed skink, give birth to live young that are wrapped in a thin membrane.

🦎 Parental care varies among lizard species; most do not provide care, while others, like the Argentine black and white tegu, show some level of parental care.

Defense Mechanisms:

🦎 Lizards have various defense mechanisms to protect themselves from predators.

🦎 Camouflage is a common tactic, allowing lizards to blend in with their environment.

🦎 Some lizards, like the horned lizard, can squirt blood from their eyes to frighten predators.

🦎 To intimidate potential threats, the frilled-neck lizard displays a large, colorful frill around its neck.

🦎 Many lizards will hiss, puff up their bodies, or perform threatening displays to make themselves appear larger and more dangerous.

Territorial Behavior:

🦎 Some lizard species, like the green anole, are territorial and will defend their territory against intruders.

🦎 Male lizards often engage in displays or physical combat to establish dominance and secure territory.

🦎 Territorial behavior is usually more pronounced during the breeding season when competition for mates is high.

Social Interactions:

🦎 Lizard's social behavior varies between species, with some being more social than others.

🦎 Individuals in social species like the green iguana may sunbake, feed, or sleep in groups. This helps them to regulate their body temperature and reduces the risk of attack by predators.

🦎 Hierarchies can form within these groups, with dominant individuals controlling food resources and mating opportunities.

🦎 The dominant lizard is in charge of everything and bobs its head to stop behavior it isn't happy with.

🦎 Some species of lizards have developed social behaviors to help them survive and reproduce.

🦎 In solitary species, social interactions are limited and usually occur during mating or territorial disputes.

- Male lizards engage in displays to attract females, such as head-bobbing, dewlap extensions (making their necks expand and stand out), or color changes.

- Some species, like the male Jackson's chameleon, have horns to impress females or fight rival males.

- Male lizards do push-ups to try to attract a female lizard. It makes them look bigger and more intimidating to the other males.

- Also, male lizards like to display their abdomen to attract females.

GEOGRAPHICAL DISTRIBUTION OF LIZARDS

🦎 Lizards have been around for over 200 million years and have adapted to a wide range of habitats and environmental conditions over that time.

🦎 Lizards have a wide range of colors, patterns, and shapes. These adaptations can help them blend into their environment and avoid predators.

🦎 Some species of lizards live in trees or other high places. These species are often adapted to life in the trees, with features such as tails that can hold things and specialized claws for gripping onto surfaces.

🦎 Lizards can also be found in a variety of different social systems, from solitary species to those that live in large groups or colonies.

LIZARDS: AN IN-DEPTH EXPLORATION

🦎 The distribution of lizards is influenced by competition with other species, predators, and resource availability.

🦎 Some species of lizards can regenerate lost body parts, such as tails or limbs. This adaptation can help them survive in environments where there are a lot of predators.

🦎 The distribution of lizards worldwide constantly changes as species evolve and adapt to new environments and the Earth's climate changes over time.

🦎 The highest diversity of lizards can be found in tropical regions, particularly in Central and South America, Southeast Asia, and Australia.

🦎 Australia and Madagascar are home to an exceptionally high number of unique lizard species, as they are isolated from other continents.

🦎 Lizards can also be found in temperate regions, such as Europe, North America, and Asia. However, their diversity is generally lower than in tropical regions.

🦎 Some species of lizards are also found in aquatic habitats, such as rivers, lakes, and oceans.

🦎 Human activities, such as habitat destruction and the introduction of non-native species, have significantly impacted lizard diversity and populations in many areas.

🦎 Some regions of the world have particularly high levels of lizard diversity. For example, the island of New Guinea, in the western Pacific, has one of the planet's highest concentrations of lizard species.

🦎 Lizards are found in a wide variety of habitats, including deserts, rainforests, grasslands, and mountains. In fact, some species of lizards can survive in extremely harsh environments, such as the gila monster, found in the deserts of the southwestern United States and Mexico.

🦎 Many species of lizards have adapted to life in desert environments by developing specialized mechanisms for conserving water. For example, some species can absorb water through their skin. In contrast, others can store water in their bodies for long periods.

🦎 In general, larger lizards tend to be found in more open habitats, while smaller lizards are more commonly found in areas with a lot of shrubs and grasses.

🦎 Some regions of the world, such as the Sahara Desert in Africa, have low levels of lizard diversity.

🦎 Historical events like continental drift influenced where lizards live. For example, the separation of South America from Africa and the formation of the Isthmus of Panama played a major role in the distribution of lizard species in the Americas.

🦎 Geological events, such as volcanic eruptions and earthquakes, affect the distribution of lizards. For example, the eruption of Mount Pinatubo in the Philippines in 1991 had a negative impact on local populations of lizards and other wildlife.

LIZARDS: AN IN-DEPTH EXPLORATION

🦎 The smallest lizards in the world are found in the Caribbean, with the dwarf gecko being one example. These tiny lizards are less than an inch long and can fit on the tip of your finger.

🦎 Some species of lizards are adapted to living in urban environments and can be found in cities around the world. For instance, the common house gecko is often found in homes and buildings in tropical regions.

🦎 Some regions of the world have been particularly impacted by the introduction of non-native species of lizards, which can negatively affect native species and ecosystems.

🦎 The brown anole, which is native to the Caribbean, has become an invasive species in Florida, where it competes with and preys upon native species of lizards.

🦎 The distribution of lizards is also influenced by the availability of food and prey. For example, some species of lizards feed on insects, while others can take down much larger prey, such as small mammals and birds.

🦎 In the American Southwest, lizards are an important part of the local ecology. They are even considered cultural icons by some indigenous groups.

🦎 Some species of lizards have been introduced to new regions of the world by humans, intentionally or accidentally. These introduced species can have negative impacts on native ecosystems and wildlife.

🦎 Some species of lizards can change color to blend in with their environment or communicate with other members of their species. This adaptation is pervasive in chameleons.

🦎 Lizards can be found in a wide range of sizes, from tiny species that can fit on the head of a pin to massive species that can weigh over 200 pounds (90 kg).

ADAPTATIONS OF LIZARDS TO DIFFERENT ENVIRONMENTS

Lizards are a diverse group of reptiles that inhabit various environments, from arid deserts to rainforests. They have developed a range of adaptations that allow them to thrive in these different environments.

Here are some of the adaptations of lizards to different environments:

Desert Variations

🦎 Many desert lizards have developed a flattened body shape that allows them to move quickly across the sand without sinking.

🦎 They also have tough, scaly skin that protects them from the harsh desert environment.

🦎 Some desert lizards can absorb water through their skin, allowing them to survive in areas where water is scarce.

🦎 Many desert lizards are active during the cooler parts of the day. They can regulate their body temperature to avoid overheating.

LIZARDS: AN IN-DEPTH EXPLORATION

- Desert-dwelling lizards, like the sandfish skink, have specialized scales that allow them to "swim" through the soft sand.

Rainforest Variations

- Lizards in rainforests have adapted to live in the humid, tropical environment.
- Many have bright colors that help them blend in with their surroundings and avoid predators.
- Some species have developed prehensile tails that allow them to grip onto branches and move easily through the trees.
- Rainforest lizards can also climb and jump easily, allowing them to move quickly through the dense vegetation.

Grassland Variations

- Lizards that live in grasslands blend in with their surroundings, making them less visible to predators.
- They often have a slim, streamlined body shape that allows them to move quickly through the grass.
- Some species have long legs that allow them to run at high speeds and escape predators.
- Grassland lizards can also burrow into the ground to avoid extreme temperatures and seek shelter.

Mountain Variations

🦎 Lizards that live in mountainous regions have adapted to the cooler temperatures and high altitudes.

🦎 Many have developed a thicker skin to retain heat and avoid dehydration.

🦎 Some species have flattened bodies that allow them to absorb heat more efficiently from the sun.

🦎 Mountain lizards are also able to climb steep surfaces and jump over gaps, allowing them to navigate the rugged terrain.

Aquatic Variations

🦎 Some lizards have adapted to aquatic environments and are able to swim and hunt underwater.

🦎 Aquatic lizards, like the water dragon, have flattened bodies and long tails that help them move quickly through the water.

🦎 They also have webbed feet and can hold their breath for extended periods of time to hunt for prey underwater.

Arctic Variations

🦎 Lizards that live in the Arctic have developed a range of adaptations to survive in the extreme cold.

🦎 Some species have the ability to change the color of their skin to match their surroundings and avoid predators.

🦎 Arctic lizards also have thicker skin and fur-like scales that help retain heat.

🦎 They can also hibernate during the winter months when food is scarce, and temperatures are too cold for them to be active.

🦎 Some lizards, like the Alpine newt, can tolerate freezing temperatures by producing antifreeze compounds in their blood.

Arid Variations

🦎 Lizards that live in arid environments, such as the Gila monster, have developed a range of adaptations to conserve water.

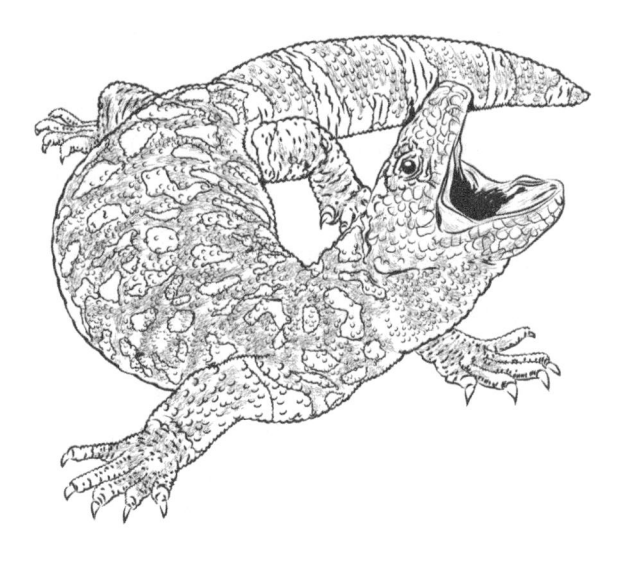

Gila Monster

🦎 They can store water in their bodies and go long periods without drinking.

🦎 The gila monster stores fat in its tail, allowing it to survive prolonged periods without food.

🦎 Arid lizards also have efficient kidneys that allow them to extract as much water as possible from their food.

🦎 Lizards living in dry environments have developed ways to collect water from their environment, such as absorbing moisture through their skin.

🦎 They also have a unique gait that allows them to move efficiently while conserving energy.

Camouflage Variations

🦎 Many lizards have developed camouflage adaptations that help them blend in with their surroundings and avoid predators.

🦎 They have evolved a range of colors and patterns that match the environment they live in.

🦎 Some species can also change the color of their skin within seconds to match their surroundings and avoid detection.

🦎 Incredibly, this color change is not just to camouflage, but it also can show body temperature, emotion and helps lizards to communicate.

Arboreal Variations

🦎 Arboreal lizards, like chameleons, have adapted to live in trees and other high-altitude environments.

🦎 Their prehensile tails allow them to grip branches and move easily through the trees.

LIZARDS: AN IN-DEPTH EXPLORATION

🦎 Their toes are also adapted to grip onto surfaces, making it easier for them to climb trees and avoid predators.

🦎 Some species of arboreal lizards, like geckos, have developed sticky toe pads that allow them to walk on vertical surfaces and even upside down.

Omnivorous Variations

🦎 Many lizards are omnivorous, which means they eat both plants and animals.

🦎 These lizards have a wide variety of teeth shapes and sizes to help them eat different types of food.

🦎 Omnivorous lizards, like the green iguana, have also developed a longer digestive tract to help them break down plant material.

Predatory Variations

🦎 Lizards are also well-known predators, and many species have developed unique adaptations to help them hunt and catch prey.

🦎 Some species, such as the chameleon, have long, sticky tongues that they use to catch insects and other small prey.

🦎 Other predatory lizards, like the Komodo dragon, have powerful jaws and sharp teeth that they use to catch and kill larger prey.

🦎 Predatory lizards have also developed good eyesight and hearing to help them locate and track their prey.

Defensive Variations

🦎 Lizards have also developed a range of defensive adaptations to protect themselves from predators.

🦎 Some species, like the horned lizard, have spiky skin that makes them difficult to swallow.

🦎 Other species, like the skink, can detach their tail as a distraction to predators and then regenerate it later.

🦎 Many lizards can also change the color of their skin or inflate their bodies to make themselves look larger and more intimidating.

Burrowing Variations

🦎 Some lizards, like the sand lizard, have adapted to live in underground burrows to avoid predators and extreme temperatures.

🦎 These lizards have strong limbs and a streamlined body shape, making digging and navigating through tunnels easy.

🦎 Some burrowing lizards also have specialized scales on their belly that help them grip the soil and move more efficiently.

Thermal Variations

🦎 Lizards are ectothermic and rely on external heat sources to regulate their body temperature.

LIZARDS: AN IN-DEPTH EXPLORATION

🦎 Some lizards, like the Gila monster, can bask in the sun to raise their body temperature. In contrast, others, like the night lizard, are active only during cooler times of the day.

🦎 Some species, like the bearded dragon, have special heat-sensing organs on their skin that allow them to detect temperature changes and locate heat sources.

Regeneration Variations

🦎 Some lizards have developed the ability to regenerate lost body parts, such as their tails or limbs.

🦎 When threatened by a predator, some species, like the gecko, can detach their tail as a distraction and regenerate it later.

🦎 The tail wiggles for up to 30 minutes and distracts the predator so the lizard can escape.

🦎 Detaching the tail can be painful and stressful for the lizard.

🦎 It can take up to 60 days to regrow the tail.

🦎 Some lizards who detach their tails frequently can regrow multiple tails.

🦎 Other species, like the green anole, can regenerate lost limbs through a process called epimorphic regeneration.

🦎 Scientists are discovering that lizards can also regenerate organs like the heart and brain.

Hibernation and Estivation Variations

🦎 Many lizards survive periods of extreme temperatures or limited food availability by entering into periods of hibernation or estivation.

🦎 During hibernation, lizards lower their metabolic rate and reduce their activity level to conserve energy during winter.

🦎 During estivation, lizards enter a period of inactivity during the hot, dry months of the year, reducing their water and energy consumption.

Camouflage and Mimicry Variations

🦎 Many lizards have developed adaptations to blend in with their environment and avoid detection by predators.

🦎 Some species, like the chameleon, can change the color of their skin to match their surroundings and avoid detection.

🦎 Other species, like the sand lizard, have evolved a coloration that matches the sand or soil in their habitat.

🦎 Some lizards have also developed mimicry adaptations, where they resemble other species to avoid being eaten.

🦎 For example, the Mexican beaded lizard has a similar coloration and pattern to the venomous Gila monster, allowing it to avoid being attacked by predators.

TYPES OF LIZARDS

1. Geckos

Examples: leopard gecko, crested gecko, day gecko

Characteristics:

🦎 Small to medium-sized lizards

🦎 Sticky toe pads for climbing

🦎 Nocturnal or diurnal depending on the species

🦎 Wide variety of colors and patterns

2. Iguanas

Examples: green iguana, marine iguana, desert iguana

Characteristics:

🦎 Large herbivorous lizards

- Long tails for balance and defense
- Green iguana: arboreal, lives in trees
- Marine iguana: unique, swims in the ocean to feed on algae
- Desert iguana: adapted to hot, arid environments

3. Chameleons

Examples: veiled chameleon, panther chameleon, Jackson's chameleon

Characteristics:

- Known for the ability to change color
- Eyes can move independently, allowing 360-degree vision
- Unique feet for grasping branches
- Slow-moving and well-camouflaged

4. Skinks

Examples: blue-tongue skink, five-lined skink, fire skink

Characteristics:

- Smooth, shiny scales
- Small legs, some species have no legs
- Active and fast-moving
- Omnivorous, eat insects, fruits, and vegetables

LIZARDS: AN IN-DEPTH EXPLORATION

5. Monitors

Examples: komodo dragon, Nile monitor, Savannah monitor

Characteristics:

- 🦎 Largest lizards in the world
- 🦎 Powerful limbs for digging and climbing
- 🦎 Forked tongue for smelling
- 🦎 Sharp teeth and claws for hunting

6. Anoles

Examples: green anole, Cuban anole, knight anole

Characteristics:

- 🦎 Small, arboreal lizards
- 🦎 Change the color from green to brown for camouflage
- 🦎 Dewlap, a throat fan for communication
- 🦎 Agile and quick-moving

7. Agamas

Examples: bearded dragon, African rainbow agama, Eastern collared lizard

Characteristics:

- 🦎 Spiny scales along the back
- 🦎 Bearded-colored males and females are duller.

8. Gila Monsters and Beaded Lizards

Examples: gila monster, Mexican bearded lizard

Characteristics:

🦎 Only venomous lizards in the world

🦎 Thick, stocky bodies with bead-like scales

🦎 Brightly colored patterns for warning predators

🦎 Slow-moving and primarily nocturnal

9. Legless Lizards

Examples: European glass lizard, California legless lizard

Characteristics:

🦎 Lack limbs, resembling snakes

🦎 Rigid, movable eyelids and external ear openings (unlike snakes)

🦎 Can detach tails when threatened

🦎 Burrowers, found in various habitats

10. Horned Lizards

Examples: Texas horned lizard, regal horned lizard, coast horned lizard

Characteristics:

🦎 Short, wide bodies with spiny scales

- Horn-like projections on their heads
- Camouflage with desert environments
- Primarily eat ants and other insects

Horned Lizard

11. Tegus

Examples: Argentine black and white tegu, red tegu, blue tegu

Characteristics:

- Large, intelligent lizards
- Omnivorous diet, including fruits, vegetables, and small animals
- Powerful limbs and tail
- Some species, like the Argentine black and white tegu, are popular pets.

12. Alligator Lizards

Examples: Northern alligator lizard, Southern alligator lizard, Mexican alligator lizard

Characteristics:

- Long, slender bodies and pointy snouts
- Scales resemble those of alligators
- Found in various habitats, from forests to grasslands
- Carnivorous, eating insects and small animals

13. Wall Lizards

Examples: Common wall lizard, Italian wall lizard, moorish wall lizard

Characteristics:

- Small, agile lizards
- Often found basking on rocks, walls, or other vertical surfaces
- Insectivorous diet
- Vibrant coloration, especially in males

14. Night Lizards

Examples: granite night lizard, Yucatan night lizard, Texas night lizard

Characteristics:

- Small, nocturnal lizards
- Cryptic coloration for camouflage
- Prefer rocky habitats with crevices for hiding
- Feed on insects and other small invertebrates

15. Plated Lizards

Examples: giant plated lizard, Sudan plated lizard, yellow-throated plated lizard

Characteristics:

- Armor-like plates on their backs
- Primarily herbivorous, with some insects in their diet
- Large, flat heads and strong limbs for burrowing
- Found in rocky and arid habitats

16. Whiptail Lizards

Examples: six-lined racerunner, desert grassland whiptail, checkered whiptail

Characteristics:

- Long, slender bodies and whip-like tails
- Fast runners, often found in open areas
- Primarily insectivorous
- Some species reproduce through parthenogenesis (females laying unfertilized eggs)

17. Flying Dragons

Examples: common flying dragon, Bornean flying dragon, Philippine flying dragon

Characteristics:

🦎 Small, arboreal lizards with wing-like structures called patagia

🦎 Glide from tree to tree for mobility and escape from predators

🦎 Colorful and well-camouflaged

🦎 Feed on insects and small invertebrates

18. Frilled Lizards

Example: Australian frilled lizard

Characteristics:

🦎 Unique frill around the neck, used for defense and communication

🦎 Run on hind legs when threatened

🦎 Arboreal and well-camouflaged

🦎 Insectivorous and occasionally eat small vertebrates

19. Basilisk Lizards

Examples: common basilisk, plumed basilisk, red-headed basilisk

Characteristics:

🦎 Known as "Jesus Christ Lizards" for their ability to run on water

🦎 Long, slender bodies and crests on the head and back

🦎 Fast runners and strong swimmers

🦎 Insectivorous and omnivorous depending on the species

20. Gecko Lizards

Examples: tokay gecko, giant leaf-tailed gecko, satanic leaf-tailed gecko

Characteristics:

🦎 Large, nocturnal geckos with unique appearances

🦎 Sticky toe pads for climbing

🦎 Camouflage to blend with their surroundings

🦎 Primarily insectivorous

WILD FACTS ABOUT THEIR BODIES

🦎 Skin shedding: Lizards shed their skin periodically to allow for growth and to remove parasites, a process called ecdysis.

🦎 Scales: Lizards are covered in scales made of keratin, which provide protection and help prevent water loss.

🦎 Tongue types: Lizards have different kinds of tongues depending on their diet; some have sticky tongues to catch insects, while others have forked tongues to sense chemical cues.

🦎 Eyesight: Lizards have excellent eyesight, with some species being able to see ultraviolet light, which helps them find food and avoid predators.

🦎 Unique reproductive methods: Lizards have various ways of reproducing, from laying eggs (oviparous) to giving live birth (viviparous) and even reproducing without a mate (parthenogenesis).

🦎 Hearing: Most lizards have external ear openings, allowing them to detect sounds and vibrations in their environment. However, they generally have a limited hearing range compared to mammals.

🦎 Parietal eye: A few lizard species have a parietal eye, also known as a "third eye," which is a light-sensitive organ on the top of their head that helps them detect changes in light and temperature.

🦎 Venomous lizards: Some lizards, like the gila monster and the Mexican bearded lizard, are venomous and use their venom to subdue prey or defend themselves.

🦎 Diverse habitats: Lizards can be found in a wide range of habitats, from deserts and forests to grasslands and even urban areas, showcasing their adaptability.

🦎 Social behaviors: Lizards exhibit various social behaviors, including territorial displays, courtship rituals, and even forming loose social groups in some species.

🦎 Gecko toe pads: Geckos have specialized toe pads with millions of tiny hair-like structures called setae, which allow them to cling to surfaces and even walk on ceilings and glass.

🦎 Frilled-neck lizards: These Australian lizards are known for their large, frilled neck that can expand when threatened, making them appear larger to predators.

🦎 **Marine iguanas**: Found in the Galápagos Islands, marine iguanas are the only lizard species that can swim and forage for food in the ocean, primarily feeding on algae.

🦎 **Basilisk lizards**: Also known as the "Jesus Christ lizard," they can run on water for short distances by rapidly moving their legs, allowing them to escape predators.

🦎 **Size variation**: Lizards range significantly in size, from the tiny dwarf gecko at 0.6 inches (16mm) to the massive komodo dragon, which can reach over 10 feet (3 meters).

🦎 **Mimicry**: Some lizard species, like the spider-tailed horned viper, have evolved unique body parts that mimic other animals, such as insects, to attract their prey.

🦎 **Longevity**: Lizards have varying lifespans depending on the species, with some living just a few years and others, like the tuatara, living up to 100 years or more.

🦎 **Olfactory senses**: Lizards have a highly developed sense of smell, using their forked tongue to pick up scent particles and transfer them to a special organ in the roof of their mouth called the Jacobson's organ.

🦎 **Parental care**: While most lizards lay eggs and provide little to no parental care, some species, like the blue-tongue skink, give birth to live young and stay with them for a short time.

🦎 **Camouflage expert**: the leaf-tailed gecko resembles a dead leaf. It is almost impossible for a predator to spot it.

LIZARDS: AN IN-DEPTH EXPLORATION

* Crested geckos: These popular pet lizards have a distinctive crest that runs from their eyes down their back, and they can jump or glide short distances using the skin flaps on their sides.

* Moloch or thorny devil: A unique Australian lizard, the thorny devil is covered in spines for defense and has a specialized skin surface that can absorb water through capillary action.

* Flying or gliding lizards: Some lizards, like the Draco genus, have developed skin flaps called patagia that allow them to glide from tree to tree, increasing their mobility and ability to escape predators.

* Prehensile tails: Many arboreal lizards, such as chameleons and some geckos, have prehensile tails that act like a fifth limb, providing extra grip while climbing and navigating their environment.

* Legless lizards: Although they may resemble snakes, legless lizards are a separate group of lizards that have evolved to lose their limbs for better burrowing or slithering through their habitats.

* Color vision: Unlike most mammals, many lizards have well-developed color vision, enabling them to see a wide range of colors to help them find food, mates, and avoid predators.

* Vocalizations: While lizards are generally thought to be silent, some species, like the gecko, can produce a range of sounds, including chirps, clicks, and barks, to communicate with other lizards.

🦎 Lizard intelligence: Some lizards, like monitor lizards, have shown signs of problem-solving abilities and even the capacity to count, indicating a higher level of intelligence than previously thought.

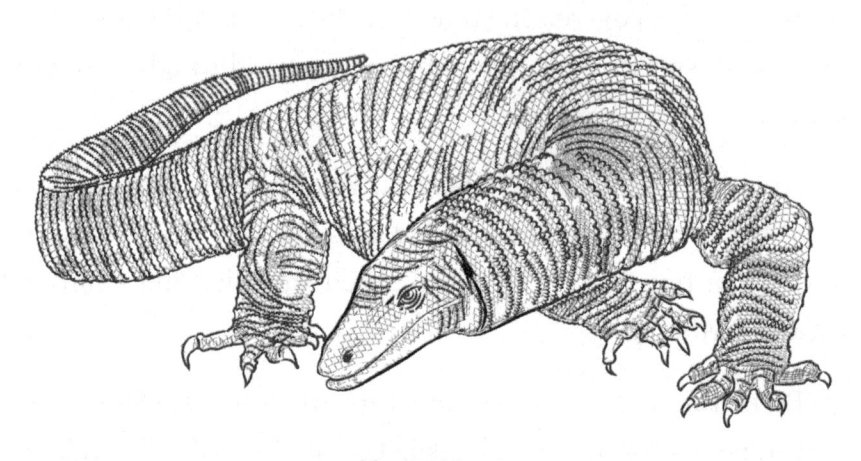

Monitor Lizard

🦎 Endemic species: Certain lizard species are found only in specific regions or on particular islands, such as the marine iguana in the Galápagos Islands or the Uroplatus geckos in Madagascar, highlighting the importance of preserving these unique ecosystems.

🦎 Sensitive to climate change: Lizards, being ectothermic, are particularly sensitive to changes in climate, with rising temperatures affecting their behavior, reproduction, and overall survival.

🦎 Lizards as bioindicators: Due to their sensitivity to environmental changes, lizards can act as bioindicators, providing valuable information about ecosystems' health and climate change's effects.

🦎 Lizards in mythology: Many cultures around the world have included lizards in their myths, legends, and folklore, often symbolizing transformation, rebirth, or cunning.

🦎 Lizard-inspired technology: Researchers have looked to lizards, such as geckos, for inspiration in developing new technologies, including adhesive materials and robotics.

🦎 Lizards in the pet trade: Some lizard species are popular as pets, like bearded dragons and leopard geckos. However, it is essential to ensure responsible sourcing and care to protect wild populations and animal welfare.

🦎 Lizards as pest control: Many lizards, particularly insectivorous species, play an important role in natural pest control, helping to keep insect populations in check.

🦎 Ecomorphs: In some ecosystems, like the Caribbean islands, different lizard species or populations have evolved similar adaptations to fill specific ecological niches, a phenomenon known as ecomorphs.

🦎 Joint relationships: Lizards can form friendly relationships with other organisms, such as the cleaner fish that remove parasites from marine iguanas or ants that protect the eggs of some gecko species.

🦎 Lizards in art and literature: Lizards have been depicted in various forms of art and literature throughout history, often symbolizing transformation, wisdom, or stealth.

🦎 Urban adaptability: Some lizard species, like the common wall lizard or green anole, have adapted to living in urban environments, using human-made structures and benefitting from the heat islands created by cities.

🦎 Lizards as food: In some cultures, lizards are consumed as food, either as a delicacy or a survival resource, providing protein and other nutrients.

🦎 Lizards in research: Lizards are used in various scientific research fields, including genetics, physiology, ecology, and evolutionary biology, due to their unique adaptations and biological characteristics.

🦎 Lizard migrations: Some lizard species, like the green iguana, have been known to migrate, often in response to changes in weather, food availability, or breeding opportunities.

🦎 Lizards and parasites: Like many animals, lizards can host a range of parasites, such as ticks, mites, and nematodes, which can impact their health and even influence their behavior.

🦎 Threats from invasive species: Lizards can face threats from invasive species, such as the brown tree snake in Guam, which has decimated local lizard populations and disrupted the island's ecosystem.

🦎 Island gigantism: Some island-dwelling lizards have evolved to be significantly larger than their mainland relatives, a phenomenon known as island gigantism, like the giant Fijian banded iguana.

LIZARDS: AN IN-DEPTH EXPLORATION

🦎 Island dwarfism: Conversely, some island-dwelling lizards have evolved to be smaller than their mainland relatives, a phenomenon known as island dwarfism, like the pygmy leaf chameleons of Madagascar.

🦎 Lizards in space: In 2013, a Russian research satellite carried geckos into space to study the effects of microgravity on their reproduction and development, providing valuable information for future space travel.

🦎 Lizards and climate adaptation: Some lizard species have developed adaptations to cope with extreme climates, such as the Saharan sandfish, which "swims" through the desert sand to avoid extreme heat.

🦎 Lizard communication: Lizards use various forms of communication, including visual displays, such as body posture or color changes, as well as sounds and chemical cues, to interact with other lizards.

🦎 Parental care exceptions: While most lizard species provide little to no parental care, there are exceptions, like the five-lined skink, which guards its nest and may even help regulate nest temperature.

🦎 Lizards as predators: Many lizards, like the Komodo dragon, are effective predators, using their speed, stealth, and powerful bite to capture and subdue their prey.

🦎 Lizards as prey: Lizards are a food source for various animals, including birds, mammals, snakes, and even other lizards, playing a crucial role in the food chain.

🦎 Lizards and human interaction: In some areas, lizards and humans live in close proximity, with the reptiles often being viewed as either helpful, due to their pest control abilities or as nuisances if they disrupt human activities.

🦎 Lizards in zoos and conservation: Many zoos and conservation organizations work to protect and study lizard species, often participating in breeding programs and research initiatives to help preserve these unique reptiles.

🦎 Lizards and temperature-dependent sex determination: Some lizard species, like the bearded dragon, reveal temperature-dependent sex determination, meaning the incubation temperature of their eggs can influence the offspring's sex.

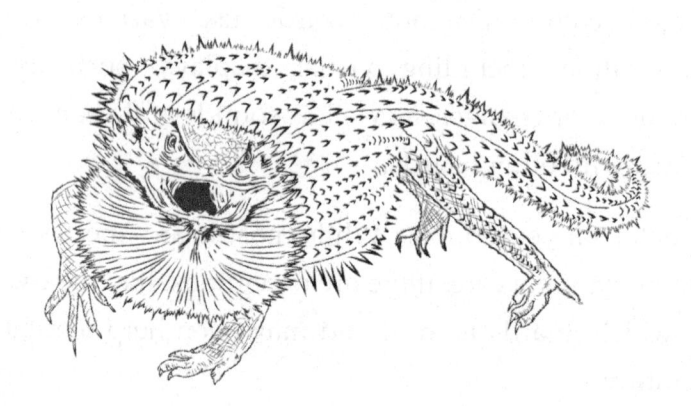

Bearded Dragon

🦎 Lizards and balance: Lizards rely on their tails for balance while running or climbing, and in some cases, they can even use their tails to help steer during jumps or glides.

LIZARDS: AN IN-DEPTH EXPLORATION

🦎 Lizards and their environment: The diversity and distribution of lizard species can be influenced by factors such as temperature, humidity, vegetation, and available food sources, with different species occupying specific niches within their habitats.

🦎 Lizards and hibernation: Some lizard species, particularly those living in colder climates, undergo a period of hibernation or brumation, a state of reduced metabolic activity to survive the winter months.

🦎 Lizards and social hierarchy: In some species, like the green anole, lizards establish social hierarchies, with dominant males controlling territories and access to resources such as food and mates.

🦎 Lizards and UV light: Many daytime lizards need exposure to ultraviolet (UV) light, which helps them combine vitamin D3, essential for calcium absorption and healthy bone growth.

🦎 Lizards and hydration: Lizards can absorb moisture through their skin and have specialized nasal glands to excrete excess salt.

🦎 Lizards and disease: Lizards can carry and transmit diseases to other animals, including humans, such as Salmonella bacteria, making it essential to practice proper hygiene when handling lizards or their habitats.

🦎 Lizards in agriculture: Some lizard species, like the common agama, can benefit agricultural areas by consuming insect pests, reducing the need for chemical pesticides and supporting sustainable farming practices.

🦎 Lizards and tourism: Lizards can be a draw for ecotourism, with travelers visiting specific locations to observe unique species, like the marine iguanas in the Galápagos Islands, boosting local economies while promoting conservation awareness.

🦎 Lizards and ecosystem health: Lizards play an essential role in maintaining the balance of ecosystems by serving as both predators and prey and contributing to processes such as seed scattering and pest control.

🦎 Lizards and cultural significance: Lizards have held various cultural meanings in different societies, with some cultures regarding them as symbols of good luck, while others view them as omens of misfortune or death.

🦎 Lizards and sensory perception: Lizards have well-developed senses, including sight, hearing, smell, and touch, which enable them to navigate their environments, find food, and avoid predators.

🦎 Lizards and their diets: Lizard diets can range from insectivorous, consuming insects and other small invertebrates, to herbivorous, eating plant materials, or even omnivorous, feeding on both plants and animals.

🦎 Lizards and locomotion: Lizards have evolved various modes of moving around, including walking, running, climbing, burrowing, and even swimming, depending on their habitat.

🦎 Lizards and symbiotic relationships: Lizards can form symbiotic relationships with other species, such as geckos and spiders, who share their web with the gecko benefiting from the spider's prey and the spider gaining protection from the gecko's presence.

🦎 Lizards and life span: The life span of lizards can vary greatly among species, with some small lizards living only a few years, while larger species, like the komodo dragon, can live for several decades.

🦎 Lizards and nest-building: Some lizard species, like the spiny-tailed iguana, construct elaborate nests to protect their eggs, using materials like rocks, leaves, or even their own saliva to build sturdy, insulated structures.

🦎 Lizards and navigation: Lizards use a combination of landmarks, celestial cues, and possibly even magnetic fields to navigate their environments, allowing them to find food, shelter, and mates in complex and dynamic habitats.

🦎 Lizards and visual signaling: Many lizards use visual signaling, such as push-ups, head-bobbing, or dewlap extensions, to communicate with conspecifics, conveying information about their identity, social status, or intentions.

🦎 Lizards and group living: While most lizard species are solitary, some, like the desert night lizard, exhibit group living or social behavior, with individuals sharing shelters, cooperating in foraging, or forming social hierarchies.

🦎 Lizards and physiological adaptations: Lizards have evolved various physiological adaptations to cope with environmental challenges, such as specialized kidneys that help conserve water in desert species or the ability to tolerate high levels of salt in marine iguanas.

🦎 Lizards and cryptic coloration: Many lizards use cryptic coloration to blend in with their surroundings, making it difficult for predators and prey to detect them, while others, like chameleons, can rapidly change their color to match their environment.

LIZARDS AND POISON/VENOM

🦎 Most lizards are not poisonous to humans or animals.

🦎 A few lizard species are venomous, but their venom is generally not lethal to humans.

🦎 Examples of venomous lizards include the gila monster and the Mexican bearded lizard.

Gila Monster:

🦎 Found in the southwestern United States and Mexico.

🦎 Produces a venom that can cause pain, swelling, and weakness.

🦎 Bites are rare, and fatalities are even rarer.

LIZARDS: AN IN-DEPTH EXPLORATION

Mexican Bearded Lizard:

🦎 Native to Mexico and Guatemala.

🦎 Venom can cause similar symptoms as the gila monster.

🦎 Bites are uncommon and not typically fatal to humans.

Other Lizards:

🦎 Some lizards can carry bacteria, such as Salmonella, on their skin.

🦎 Handling lizards without proper hygiene can lead to illness in humans.

🦎 It is important to wash hands thoroughly after contact with any reptile.

PREDATORS THAT AFFECT LIZARDS

🦎 Many animals prey on lizards as part of their diet, making lizards an important part of the food chain.

Birds:

Birds of prey, like hawks and eagles, feed on lizards:

🦎 They have sharp talons and beaks to catch and tear their prey.

🦎 Examples: red-tailed hawk, bald eagle

Smaller birds may also eat smaller lizard species:

🦎 They snatch lizards from branches or the ground.

🦎 Examples: shrikes, roadrunners

Mammals:

Various mammals hunt lizards for food:

- 🦎 These predators rely on their agility and speed.

- 🦎 Examples: foxes, raccoons, mongoose

Some domestic animals, like cats, may also hunt lizards:

- 🦎 Cats are natural predators with strong hunting instincts.

Reptiles:

Larger reptiles, including other lizards, can be lizard predators:

- 🦎 They use their size and strength to catch prey.

- 🦎 Examples: larger monitor lizards, snakes (like king snakes)

Amphibians:

Some amphibians feed on smaller lizards:

- 🦎 Frogs and toads can catch lizards with their long, sticky tongues.

- 🦎 Examples: horned frogs, giant toads

Invertebrates:

Invertebrates like spiders and large insects can prey on small lizards:

- 🦎 They use various tactics, such as ambush or web-trapping.

- 🦎 Examples: tarantulas, praying mantises.

CATCHING FOOD AND FOOD FACTS

HOW DO THEY EAT?

Lizards have a unique feeding technique called "gape and suck."

🦎 They open their mouths wide and create suction to draw in food.

🦎 This method is especially useful for aquatic and semi-aquatic species.

Lizards have a flexible, expandable stomach

🦎 It can accommodate large meals and stretch to hold more food.

🦎 This allows lizards to eat large quantities at once, especially when food is abundant.

Lizards may eat their own shed skin

🦎 This behavior is called "dermatophagy."

🦎 It helps them recycle nutrients and reduce waste.

Lizards face various threats while eating

🦎 Predators, such as birds of prey, snakes, and mammals, may attack them.

🦎 They must remain vigilant while feeding to avoid becoming prey themselves.

Some lizard species exhibit unique feeding behaviors

🦎 The frilled-neck lizard flares its frill to scare off predators while eating.

LIZARDS IN THE NEWS

KOMODO ISLAND: HOME OF THE WORLD'S LARGEST LIZARDS

🦎 The komodo dragon is a monitor lizard and is located exclusively in Indonesia.

🦎 They have their own island called Komodo Island.

🦎 There are about 2000 lizards on Komodo Island.

🦎 The komodo is an incredible-looking lizard and is the largest species of lizard, growing up to ten feet long and weighing more than 160 pounds.

🦎 The komodo loves to hunt and has sharp claws and strong jaws. These amazing reptiles have serrated teeth and can easily hunt, tear apart and devour wild pigs, deer, water buffalo, snakes, and turtles.

🦎 They are also quite venomous. Their bite has proteins that cause uncontrollable bleeding in the prey. This lowers blood pressure, and the prey goes into shock.

🦎 The saliva from the dragon has bacteria in it as well, so the prey can get an infection before it dies. Larger animals take quite a while to die.

🦎 The venom is not fast-acting like it is with snakes.

KOMODO DRAGONS IN THE NEWS

Komodo Dragon

🦎 Although attacks on humans are rare, they do happen.

🦎 In 2007, a boy who lived on Komodo Island was attacked and died from blood loss. It was the hot, dry season, and the natural waterholes were empty, with no prey drinking there. So, the rangers believe the boy was sadly a victim of an extremely hungry Komodo.

🦎 In 2008, a group of scuba divers were caught in a strong ocean current for about 10 hours. Eventually, exhausted, they were washed up alive on what they thought was a deserted island. Wrong! They had landed on Rinca Island near Komodo Island. Rinca Island is home to around 1300 komodos. It was midnight, the attacks began almost immediately, and the group had to fight off the dragons with their water belts and rocks continuously. After two days, they were rescued, and all managed to stay alive.

THANKS

Thanks for taking the time to take a walk down the Snakes and Lizards path with me! I really hope you enjoyed reading the book.

If you enjoyed this book, please do leave a review on Amazon to let other readers know.

If you would like any learning and English tips, please follow me on Instagram at:

Grammatika.brisbane

or you can reach me from my website at:

www.grammatika.net.au

Nicole Foster

REFERENCES

1. Australian Geographic (2020). *Australia's 10 most dangerous snakes.*
2. Banzato, T., Hellebuyck, T., Caelenberg, A. V., Saunders, J. H., & Zotti, A. (2013). A review of diagnostic imaging of snakes and lizards. *Veterinary Record, 173*(2), 43-49.
3. Bartlett, P. P., Griswold, B., & Bartlett, R. D. (2001). *Reptiles, amphibians, and invertebrates.* Barron's.
4. Beatson, C., (2022). Inland Taipan. *The Australian Museum,* Accessed February 16, 2023.
5. Beck, D. D. (2005). *Biology of Gila monsters and beaded lizards* (Vol. 9). Univ of California Press.
6. Bertelsen, M. F. (2014). Squamates (snakes and lizards). *Zoo animal and wildlife immobilization and anesthesia,* 351-363.
7. Cundall, D. A. V. I. D., & Greene, H. W. (2000). Feeding in snakes. *Feeding: form, function, and evolution in tetrapod vertebrates, 9,* 293-333.
8. Farley, C. T., & Ko, T. C. (1997). Mechanics of locomotion in lizards. *The Journal of experimental biology, 200*(16), 2177-2188.
9. Feldman, A., Sabath, N., Pyron, R. A., Mayrose, I., & Meiri, S. (2016). Body sizes and diversification rates of lizards, snakes, amphisbaenians and the tuatara. *Global Ecology and Biogeography, 25*(2), 187-197.
10. FitzSimons, V. F. M. (1962). Snakes of Southern Africa. *Snakes of Southern Africa.*
11. Fry, B. G., Vidal, N., Norman, J. A., Vonk, F. J., Scheib, H., Ramjan, S. R., ... & Kochva, E. (2006). Early evolution of the venom system in lizards and snakes. *Nature, 439*(7076), 584-588.

REFERENCES

12. Gans, C. (1961). The feeding mechanism of snakes and its possible evolution. *American Zoologist*, 217-227.
13. Gray, J. (1946). The mechanism of locomotion in snakes. *Journal of experimental biology*, 23(2), 101-120.
14. Hodgson, W.C., Dal Belo, C.A., Rowan, E.G. (2007). The neuromuscular activity of paradoxin: A presynaptic neurotoxin from the venom of the inland taipan (Oxyuranus microlepidotus). *Neuropharmacology*, 52(5):1229-1236. doi:10.1016/j.neuropharm.2007.01.002
15. Koh, D. C. I., Armugam, A., & Jeyaseelan, K. (2006). Snake venom components and their applications in biomedicine. *Cellular and Molecular Life Sciences CMLS*, 63, 3030-3041.
16. Lillywhite, H. B. (2014). *How snakes work: structure, function and behavior of the world's snakes*. Oxford University Press.
17. Marais, J. (2022). *A complete guide to the snakes of southern Africa*. Penguin Random House South Africa.
18. Meier, J., & Stocker, K. F. (2017). Biology and distribution of venomous snakes of medical importance and the composition of snake venoms. In *Handbook of: Clinical Toxicology of Animal Venoms and Poisons* (pp. 367-412). CRC Press.
19. Mirtschin, P. (2006). The pioneers of venom production for Australian antivenoms. *Toxicon*, 48(7):899-918. doi:10.1016/j.toxicon.2006.07.026
20. Moon, B. R., Penning, D. A., Segall, M., & Herrel, A. (2019). Feeding in snakes: form, function, and evolution of the feeding system. *Feeding in vertebrates: Evolution, morphology, behavior, biomechanics*, 527-574.
21. Mullin, S. J., & Seigel, R. A. (Eds.). (2011). *Snakes: ecology and conservation*. Cornell University Press.
22. Newer, R. (2013). The Most Infamous Komodo Dragon Attacks of the Past 10 Years. *Smithsonian Magazine*, Accessed March 14, 2023.

REFERENCES

23. Pianka, E. R., & Vitt, L. J. (2003). *Lizards: windows to the evolution of diversity* (Vol. 5). Univ of California Press.
24. Pough, F. H. (1973). Lizard energetics and diet. *Ecology, 54*(4), 837-844.
25. Shine, R. (2003). Reproductive strategies in snakes. *Proceedings of the Royal Society of London. Series B: Biological Sciences, 270*(1519), 995-1004.
26. Tasoulis, T., & Isbister, G. K. (2017). A review and database of snake venom proteomes. *Toxins, 9*(9), 290.
27. Tu, A. T. (1973). Neurotoxins of animal venoms: snakes. *Annual review of biochemistry, 42*(1), 235-258.
28. Van Dyke, J. U., Thompson, M. B., Burridge, C. P., Castelli, M. A., Clulow, S., Dissanayake, D. S., ... & Whittington, C. M. (2021). Australian lizards are outstanding models for reproductive biology research. *Australian Journal of Zoology, 68*(4), 168-199.

Made in the USA
Las Vegas, NV
07 November 2023